What peop

Parenting is a challenge at the best of times. And how much more so when not one but two of your children experience serious, chronic health issues? When long, sleepless nights and endless days spent in doctor's offices and hospitals drive you to the brink of exhaustion and despair? But it is there, at the brink—as Sandra Wallis can attest—that God meets us. Where we experience His unfathomable strength, mercy, grace, and love. This isn't simply the story of heroic parents and determined, courageous children. It is, above all, the story of a God who sees, a God who cares. And a God whose faithful presence allows us to not only survive fiery trials, but to experience true peace, joy, and hope in the midst of them.

—Sara Davison
Award-winning author of *The Seven Trilogy*
and *The Night Guardians Series*

An epic story of infinitely hard work, sharing, and faith. I was involved professionally with this family for many years, and was amazed at the devotion to two handicapped children by their parents. I still see Darryl working away as a pharmacist despite his huge surgeries a few years ago! May the Lord continue to smile upon you all.

—Dr. Ian M. Connor
Wallis family pediatrician

After reading your story, I cannot help but feel an incredible sense of awe and pride to have you as my friend. The challenges you have faced are more than I can conceive. Writing these pages must have been painful as you relived the past—yet fulfilling, in knowing you faced it with great strength, wisdom, and determination. Your resourcefulness, deep love, and faith have been instilled in your children as they face their own personal challenges. Your book is a compelling and inspirational story of strength and determination to give the very best to your family. Giving up is not an option. You and Wayne are amazing.

—Maureen
Retired RN

I had the privilege of meeting this incredible lady when her children were all still at home, and I was immediately struck with her gracious and delightfully energetic personality. I knew I was in the presence of an amazing woman! She was always willing to come alongside and help with any requests I had, despite the very challenging load she carried every day.

It was only later that I learned the extent of her struggles in raising four young children, two of whom were physically challenged. One of her children suffered from spina bifida, and another had a very severe illness that required many hours of medical attention each day. Despite these very heavy demands on her time, Sandra always made time for others and never dwelt on her own problems.

At a later date, I asked Sandra, "How do you carry on?" Her astounding reply was, "It's just part of motherhood, and God always gives His grace to endure and never gives more than one can handle."

Her incredibly positive attitude in every situation has shone brilliantly throughout all her years of child-rearing. Sandra believes that having a daughter with a chronic illness caused her to rely and trust in God in ways that she never would have thought possible. She would tell you that her daughter and son who required more attention than her other children have taught her the power of compassion, a positive attitude, and true bravery.

Those who have had the privilege of calling Sandra a dear friend are blessed indeed. Personally, she has helped me deal with the difficulties in my life with confidence and a positive outlook. Sandra's example of living joyously despite the adversities of life has given me and many others the strength and courage to face the inevitable life struggles we encounter. Sandra tells everyone she encounters that with faith we can withstand any trials we may face and triumph over the storms of life. She has enabled me to deal with my own problems, however small or large they may be, and to move from a negative outlook to a positive one.

I highly recommend this book to you, and I trust her example of a positive outlook on life will be an inspiration to you as it has been to me. This is a book that everyone should read!

—Marilyn Burr
Friend

NOT
WHAT I
BARGAINED
FOR

NOT WHAT I BARGAINED FOR

My Journey Raising
Four Incredible Kids,
Including Two with Severe
Medical Conditions

Sandra Wallis

NOT WHAT I BARGAINED FOR
Copyright © 2020 by Sandra Wallis

The poem "11 Things I Wish my Child's Doctor Knew" by Anna Jaworski is reprinted with permission of Baby Hearts Press.

Scripture marked NIV taken from the Holy Bible, NEW INTERNATIONAL VERSION®, NIV® Copyright © 1973, 1978, 1984, 2011 by Biblica, Inc.® Used by permission. All rights reserved worldwide. • Scripture marked NKJV taken from the New King James Version®, Copyright © 1982 by Thomas Nelson, Inc. Used by permission. All rights reserved.

The content of this publication is based on actual events. Names may have been changed to protect individual privacy.

ISBN: 978-1-4866-1934-4
eBook ISBN: 978-1-4866-1935-1

Word Alive Press
119 De Baets Street Winnipeg, MB R2J 3R9
www.wordalivepress.ca

WORD ALIVE
—P R E S S—

Cataloguing in Publication information can be obtained from Library and Archives Canada.

This book is dedicated to my husband, Wayne. I could never have survived this journey without your help. You are my rock.

"For I know the plans I have for you" declares the Lord "
plans to prosper you and not to harm you,
plans to give you hope and a future."
(Jeremiah 29:11, NIV)

Acknowledgements

*N*ot *What I Bargained For* wouldn't have been possible without the encouragement and support of so many wonderful people. It's almost impossible to thank each one individually, but there are a few who have stood out over the years of writing this book.

Ann Brent, a writer herself, for continually telling me that this story needed to be told.

Marilyn Burr, a retired teacher, who was often at my door with presents for Darryl and our family as well as uplifting cards, and who encouraged me to help others through our story of hope.

Dr. Ian Connor, our pediatrician, who kept our children alive with his expert care.

The staff at Calea Pharmacy who talked to me weekly and supplied all Darryl's medical needs. Eve Harper, customer service representative, was like a therapist, always believing that I could cope with the life and death situations I was facing every day.

Ontario Ostomy, who also supplied all the ostomy supplies for Heather and Darryl.

My close friends in Toronto while I was at the hospital with Darryl who listened to my concerns. Among them, my best friend Judy Falkner who visited us often and brought gifts for Darryl and took me out for lunch—a much-needed break away from the hospital and who offered a quiet place to stay. My childhood friend Maureen, retired nurse, who could understand what I was going through on a daily basis.

The nurses and doctors at the Hospital for Sick Children and the Toronto General Hospital who were patient with me while I learned to care for Darryl. The nurses and doctors at Sarnia General Hospital who cared for Darryl when it was possible for him to be treated locally.

The Ronald McDonald house in London and Toronto for providing me an affordable, beautiful place to stay, as well as meals.

The recreational staff at the hospital that kept Darryl's mind off all the procedures he had to have by bringing him toys like Lego. Bunky the Clown brought a smile to Darryl's face, even on the darkest days. Marnie's lounge, where Darryl spent many hours playing pool and making crafts. Volunteers, like Dorothy in the playroom, who would just talk to me and rock Darryl so I could get out for a walk by myself.

My many friends, including our church family, who brought meals and babysat the other children while I was away at the hospital with either Darryl or Heather. I thank you for your kindness and thoughtfulness. Churches who prayed worldwide for our family. Friends like Kathryn Cornelisse and Debbie Smith, who called to let me know they were there for us—anytime, day or night.

Pastor Wayne Domm and his wife Dayle, who prayed with us many times and taught us about God and Jesus through heartfelt sermons.

My homemaker from the Red Cross, Margaret Druiett, who taught me to be consistent with the children and helped me keep the house in order when chaos abounded.

Helen Henderson, who made our trip to England possible by writing an article in *The Toronto Star* newspaper. Sandra and Graham Goldcrown from England, who went out of their way to make our trip memorable, helping us immensely with the details and the driving.

The transplant team at the Toronto General Hospital who worked tirelessly night and day to keep Darryl alive.

The many agencies that helped us out financially, including the Easter Seal Society, the March of Dimes, the Ministry of Community and Social Service, and the Shriners. Without their help our lives would have been very different. The Make a Wish and Sunshine Foundations, who provided fun trips to Disney—all expenses paid—that all our children will never forget.

The Rotary Centre in Sarnia, ON and Thames Valley Children's Centre in London, ON for the multiple kinds of therapy and counselling services they provided to our family.

Our employers, Marriott International, New Life Mills, and Parrish and Heimbecker, who not only gave us time off to care for our children, but gifts of money, food and lodging. We will be forever in your debt.

Word Alive Press for shortlisting me in the Women's Journey of Faith contest and believing that my story should be told. Marina Reis, project manager, for her help in bringing this project to completion. And editor Matthew Knight, whose sharp eye for detail and creative mind made my book easier to read by shaping its content and flow.

My children, especially Leanne and Krystle—you had to help out and grow up way before your time.

Our parents, Mary and Emerson Wallis and Evelyan and William Wilson, who brought us up with solid Christian values and morals that shaped us into the people we are today.

I would also like to thank God for caring for our family and instilling in me the hope that everything will work out and that God will be glorified.

CONTENTS

INTRODUCTION

Special needs children take a lot of time and energy. Over the years, a lot of my friends have asked me how I've managed. The only answer I can give them is that "you just do it."

Looking back, I've wondered myself how I was able to make it through each day, but God gave me strength. Our pastor at the Evangelical Missionary Church said in a sermon one Sunday that trials and tribulations make us stronger, and we learn from these experiences. God refines us this way, he said. I often thought God could have taught me a different way, but I trusted Him from the very beginning.

When you're physically sick with a head cold or the flu, you often feel like you're dying. When you're dealing with the problems of everyday life, you feel you're the only one. But in reality, everyone has something they are going through—it's a different situation, but that doesn't mean it feels easier.

My friends would often tell me about their children having colds or the flu and how hard it was, and then they would look at my situation and apologize for complaining. But it's all relative—colds or the flu might be monumental to them, whereas being up all night with a sick child who had been vomiting for hours and was now dehydrated was what I was dealing with.

One problem isn't greater than the other—it's just different. Everyone is dealing with something, and we must trust that God is in control and can get us through anything.

This is the true story of my family and how we all survived and thrived. It is very hard to relive this journey—I've often found myself in tears as I write—but I'm writing this in the hope that it will help someone else going through a similar situation.

FOREWORD

It is my honour and privilege to call Sandra—Sandy—my friend. Sandra has a tenacious spirit like no one I've ever met. As you read of the heartaches and triumphs she and her family have experienced, you will find yourself wanting to reach out to hug and encourage her. You will be amazed at the strength God has bestowed upon this special woman and her family.

I have known Sandra, and her husband Wayne, for more than forty years. We've shared many of life's struggles and joys—walking together through our pregnancies, raising our babies, and seeing them mature and leave the nest. And I've stood with Sandra as she has faced life-threatening decisions many times regarding her children.

Sandra and Wayne's second child, Heather, was born with spina bifida, and doctors said she would never walk. I vividly recall Sandra boldly stating, with tears streaming down her face, "She *will* walk." Heather is now thirty-nine years old, and has walked unaided for years.

Their fourth baby, Darryl, was born with a rare disease called gastrointestinal pseudo-obstruction. For years, I watched Sandra in amazement as she seemed to know instinctively what her son needed, and she fought incessantly, as a mother bear for her cub, to get the specialized care Darryl required.

Sandra is a constant inspiration to me and to all who know her. This incredible woman has somehow always found the time to bake her own bread and yummy ginger cookies. She is passionate about sewing, quilting, and tending to the gorgeous poppies in her garden, and she will joyfully make a cup of tea for anyone stopping by for a visit. Sandra has boundless energy and is that person you can always count on. She is the embodiment of the saying, "If you want something done, ask a busy person."

Even in the midst of challenges that would stop most people in their tracks, Sandra and Wayne have gone above and beyond to provide a wonderful, nurturing home for their four children. With each curveball thrown into their lives, they have consistently continued to hit home runs.

Sandra's story, straight from the heart of this devoted mom, will amaze you. Not only will you see what can be accomplished through unstoppable love, commitment, and determination, but you will also have a front-row seat to a rare glimpse of God's miraculous power still at work in the world today.

—Debbie Smith
Friend

CHAPTER ONE

The Phone Call

November 27, 2006

What is that sound? It's three a.m. on Monday morning. Who could be calling in the middle of the night? I stagger to the phone, having been sound asleep only seconds before. "Hello, who is this?"

"Mom, it's me, Darryl. They called."

I press the fingers of my free hand to my temple. "Who called?"

"The hospital."

I struggle to process what he's saying. Why would the hospital call my son? My eyes widen. *Could it be?* "Do they have a donor?"

For over eight months, we've both been carrying pagers that will alert us if a donor becomes available. I've been waiting a long time for this moment. I'm excited but anxious at the same time, so many questions running through my brain—*Do they have all the organs? Are they all from one donor? Is it a good match?*

"Yes. I have to go to the hospital immediately."

My heart pounds. "We'll leave right now. Don't let the doctors take you into surgery before we get there." I don't tell him I want him to wait for us in case he doesn't survive this operation and we lose our chance to say goodbye.

My husband Wayne and I are elated and scared at the same time. Who knows what is going through Darryl's mind? He's been told he has a 50/50 chance of surviving the surgery. How can someone prepare themselves for something like that? How can we prepare ourselves for the possibility of losing our son?

We arrive at 7 a.m. Darryl sits on a hospital bed, dressed in a blue gown and ready for surgery. He looks as apprehensive as we feel.

The transplant doctor walks into the room shortly after we do. He stands at the end of the bed and meets our son's eyes steadily. "This is your only chance of survival. You may not make it. You have to decide if you are willing to take this chance."

My heart sinks. I glance at Wayne. He reaches for my hand and squeezes it.

The doctor clears his throat. "Your parents cannot make this decision for you. You are an adult now. It's up to you."

I bite my lip. Darryl is just twenty years old. In my eyes, he is so young to be making this life-changing decision. How could he ever—

"I want to do it."

I stare at my son. He sounds so confident. "Darryl, are you sure?" I ask.

He manages a small smile. "Mom, this is my only chance of survival. I'm dying."

I know the words are true, but still they strike me with the force of a ton of bricks. How is it possible that this young man, this beautiful baby of mine, could be dying? It feels like a terrible nightmare—a nightmare I've been trying to wake up from for years.

As we wait in the surgical waiting room, I begin thinking of some happier events that have led us to this point in time.

CHAPTER TWO

Wayne and I

It all began one April night many years ago in 1972 when my girlfriend and I went to Lucan, a small town with a well-known bar called the Shillelagh. We were from Toronto, so going into the country to a bar fourteen miles from London was a little scary. Toronto had lots of streetlights and houses. In the country, there was only darkness and a few scattered lights from farms in the area. I feared we would break down—there were no cellphones then.

That was the night I met Wayne. He was attending his brother's wedding downstairs, and had come upstairs to the bar with his buddies to have a beer. They came over and started talking to Leslie and me. I was attracted to Wayne's buddy and we began dating soon after. His friend and I went out for about a year. When we broke up, I realized I was actually interested in Wayne, and the two of us began to date.

Wayne had a good sense of humour, which I loved. "I like your smile," he said. Before even three weeks of going out together, I knew he was the one for me. We travelled back and forth from Toronto to Sarnia for a year. One day, when Wayne was on his way to Toronto to see me, he was in a car accident. Thankfully, he wasn't hurt, but we decided it was time to plan our wedding and for me to move to Sarnia.

I began looking for a job as a secretary in Sarnia, and found work at a company called Polysar. The same day I got that job, Wayne and I found a small apartment and painted it green and orange. *It reminds me of a pumpkin,* I remember thinking, but since we didn't have money to buy more paint, we left it.

While I worked at Polysar, Wayne worked at a feed mill in Wyoming, Ontario, a small town fifteen miles from Sarnia. Friends and family donated all sorts of furniture to us, which filled up our one-bedroom apartment. We had a clothesline in the backyard so I could hang out the wash just like I had while growing up in Toronto. We both learned how to cook. We were very happy.

We liked to go to dances in the country barns every Saturday night with his friends, who all eventually got married. In 1973, we went to Acapulco, Mexico during the Christmas before our wedding. It was the farthest Wayne had been from home. He had never been on an airplane, so it was a real adventure.

We had a nice hotel right across the road from the beach. Breakfast was included, so our day started off well with lots of fruit, freshly baked bread, and hot, rich coffee. We spent a lot of time at the beach each day. There were always vendors there selling bottles of brown oil that were supposed to be suntan lotion. I knew I would burn to a crisp if I used that, so we didn't buy any. The waves were very big, so we didn't go into the water very far. We heard that a man had died on that very beach just the week before.

Being young, we weren't afraid of anything. We decided to rent a vehicle and drive down the coast. We got a map, rented a Jeep, and off we went in shorts and T-shirts. It didn't really occur to us to prepare for the trip; we didn't bring hats or even bottles of water. As we drove past a field, we saw some men working, so we stopped to see what they were doing. Neither of us spoke Spanish, so when one of the men approached us with a machete in his hand, we were scared. Fortunately, he had a cantaloupe in his other hand, which he cut in half and gave to us. As we were hungry and thirsty, we were very happy to take it. We thanked him, and he smiled broadly.

After a brief rest, we were on our way again. Not too far down the road, we were stopped by the Mexican Army. I grabbed Wayne's arm. "Why are they stopping us?"

"I don't know, but we'd better do what they say."

Since they had big guns and had parked their jeeps across the road as a barrier, that seemed like good advice.

One of them approached the Jeep. "*Su pasaporte, por favor.*"

Wayne held up his hands. "We don't speak Spanish."

The man shook his head, a look of disgust on his face. No doubt he was thinking something along the lines of *stupid tourists*, or whatever that was in Spanish. "Passports." He held out his hand, palm up.

Wayne looked at me. I shook my head. We hadn't thought to bring water on this hot trip; it certainly hadn't occurred to us to pack the proper documents.

My stomach tightened. "Will they ask us for money?"

Wayne shrugged. "I certainly hope not, since we don't have much of that either."

After about fifteen excruciating minutes, during which the soldiers conferred with each other, they came back over to the Jeep. The one who had asked for our passports waved a hand and said, *"Andale pues."*

Thankfully, from all the John Wayne movies Wayne had watched, he knew that this meant, "Get out of here quick." We got out of there. Quick.

Relieved to have survived the close call, we relaxed and enjoyed the ride. It was a glorious sunny day and we soaked it all up. The countryside was quite barren and there were not many animals in the fields. I rested my head against the back of the seat. "I wonder how these farmers make their living."

"I have no idea." Wayne leaned over the steering wheel. "It's getting pretty dark, and it looks like only one of the headlights is working."

I straightened up and looked out the front window. The road was definitely darker on one side than the other. "Great, that's all we—"

Wayne slammed on the brakes, reaching out an arm to keep me from flying forward.

My heart pounded against my ribs. "What was that?"

"A donkey." Wayne nodded at the ditch. "I didn't see him coming. He must have seen our single headlight and turned back in time."

I'd come close to hitting a few animals in my life, but a donkey was a first for me. I managed a nervous giggle as we continued down the road, driving considerably slower now. I slumped back in my seat and was almost asleep when the Jeep shuddered and slowed to a crawl. I straightened up and peered out the front windshield. "What is it, another donkey?"

"No." The engine sputtered and chugged as Wayne manoeuvred the vehicle to the side of the road, where the vehicle promptly died. He tapped the gas gauge with the tip of one finger. "Gauge must be broken. We're out of gas."

Although night was falling, it was still extremely hot. As we'd spent the day in the sun without hats and water, we were parched. A bus, loaded with people, rumbled down the road toward us. Wayne stepped into its path and raised his arm. The driver stopped and opened the door. We tried to explain what had happened. The driver nodded, but we had no idea whether he had actually understood. Finally, he jerked his head toward the back of the bus.

Desperate to get somewhere with gas and water, Wayne and I didn't argue. Wayne held out his hand so the driver could take the required number of pesos. He took us to a small town where we went to a gas station and, with the little cash we had brought with us, we bought a jug of gasoline.

I eyed the container. "How are we going to get this to the Jeep?"

Wayne looked around. A man who looked as much like a tourist as we did was filling up his tank at another pump. Wayne strode over to him. "Hi there. Do you speak English, by any chance?"

The man finished adding the last bit of gas to his tank and replaced the nozzle. A wide grin spread across his face. "Sure do. Name's John. I'm from Michigan." He held out his hand. "My wife ..." he nodded at the woman in the passenger seat, who leaned over to smile up at us, "she's from here. We met in this town and we've come back to go to a wedding."

Wayne grasped his hand and shook it firmly. "I'm Wayne, and this is my fiancée, Sandra. We're from Ontario, Canada."

"Nice to meet you." John gestured toward the container. "Run out of gas, did you?"

"I'm afraid so." Wayne inclined his head in the direction we'd come from. "A few miles back that way, shortly after we almost ran down a donkey."

John laughed. "Welcome to Mexico." He pointed at the back seat. "The wedding is starting soon, so we don't have time to take you there now. You're welcome to come with us and spend the night at my wife's parents' house, though. We can take you wherever you need to go tomorrow."

Wayne looked at me. I lifted my shoulders. We didn't have much choice. We climbed into the back seat.

The wedding started at eleven p.m. Everyone was drinking and eating and talking in Spanish. We really felt out of place in our shorts and T-shirts. A man sort of befriended me, so Wayne stayed close. After a while I turned to John. "Do you know if that guy is married? I kind of feel like he's stalking me."

John chuckled. "No, actually, he's gay. I'm pretty sure it's Wayne he's stalking, not you."

We left the party shortly after.

The next day, John took us back to the Jeep. We filled the tank up and drove back to the resort in Acapulco. After all our wild, carefree adventures, we were very glad to get back to Canada. However, nothing could have prepared us for what was going to come.

"Mr. and Mrs. Wallis?" My thoughts scatter as I look up to see who's talking. It's a surgical nurse with an update on Darryl's progress. Perspiration drips from her forehead. "The operation is going well. Someone will come out every so often to update you on your son's progress."

We both breathe a sigh of relief that it isn't bad news.

"Do you want a coffee?" Wayne asks. "I need to get some air." Several hours have gone by, and we're getting anxious.

"Yes," I answer, thinking how happy I am that I've chosen such a thoughtful and patient person for my husband. While he's gone, I begin thinking of how God brought the two of us together, since it was very unlikely that we would have met otherwise.

CHAPTER THREE

Opposites Really Do Attract

Wayne came from a farm family of four children and I was from a city family of two children. They say opposites attract, and that we were. I knew nothing about farming. I called all cows "cows." He explained that a group of cows was referred to as "cattle," a male was a bull, and a heifer was a young cow that had never had a baby. I also learned that baby horses were called foals, not "baby horses." I knew the difference between chickens and roosters, but I had never been to a farm before.

Once, my Grade Ten class went to Albion Hills, a small town near Toronto, on a field trip. There was a farm there so city kids could learn all about the animals instead of just seeing them in books. They had a couple of cows, a few chickens, a pig, and a horse. We got to touch them through the fence. It was a good experience.

Wayne's farm had chickens, milking cows, beef cattle, and pigs—as well as horses, which his family raced. Every Saturday night his whole family would go to the racetrack in London to watch his brother Kevin race their horses. Oftentimes he would win, and the whole family would run down to the track to get their pictures taken with Kevin and the horse. They would bet on the horses as well—something that I found challenging to wrap my head around at first. When I was growing up, we'd been taught never to gamble.

Our differences were obvious to everyone. Take healthcare, for example. My dad thought it was important for us to be looked after by a specialist. "I'm not going to trust a general practitioner with my children," he used to say. The closest pediatrician was at the other side of Toronto, an hour and a half one way on a Greyhound bus. My mom would take my brother Garry and me there for check-ups and all our childhood immunizations. It was an all-day trip: we had to get up by 6:30 a.m. to catch the 8:00 a.m. bus in order to get to the office by 10:00 a.m. For me, the highlight of the visit was when we picked out a little toy or ring to take home. We looked forward to going out for lunch and shopping at the big Eaton's department store after the appointment before boarding the bus home.

If we needed medicine, the doctor would call the prescription in to our local drugstore and someone from there would deliver it on a bicycle since we didn't have a car to pick it up. When anyone in Wayne's family was sick, the doctor came to the house and brought the medicine with him.

(These memories reminded me of the many times that our pediatrician came directly to our house and right up into Darryl's room, where he lay nearly lifeless in his crib. Often the doctor would order an ambulance and Darryl would be transported to the hospital. In the 1980s, when we had our children, it was unheard of for a doctor to make house calls.)

As a kid, I played ice hockey, baseball, rode my bike everywhere, and learned how to swim. Wayne didn't play any sports and wasn't a good swimmer. He had to ride his bicycle to school in the fall, and he hated it.

Everyone knew each other in the country, even if they lived miles apart. I guess they saw each other at the grocery store, post office, or church. In the city, you hardly knew your neighbours. There were murders and robberies in the city, and people kept to themselves. Our doors were always locked. In the country, murders were rare, and people left their doors unlocked even when they were asleep at night. As time went by, thieves found out the country farm homes were not locked during the day either. Mary and Emerson, Wayne's parents, knew of neighbours who'd had their whole freezer cleaned out while they weren't at home. After that, all doors were locked day and night, as well as their freezer that was out in the barn.

One day when I was visiting the farm, the phone rang. It was a neighbour across the road.

"Where were you yesterday morning, Mary?" she asked. The neighbours watched every car that passed their house, and always waved to strangers. I would never wave to someone I didn't know—no one would ever do that in Toronto! We were raised never to talk to someone we didn't know.

Wayne's community had a weekly paper called *The St. Mary's Journal Argus*. I found the publication hilarious because it reported on such momentous events as "Sandra Wilson from Toronto visited the home of Wayne Wallis and enjoyed Sunday dinner." *How trivial*, I thought. The Toronto newspapers concentrated on stories about thefts or murders.

Wayne knew nothing about city life. I couldn't imagine streets without lights, and he was amazed at how many lights were on in the city all night long. There were homeless people on the streets in Toronto, and Wayne wasn't street smart. He didn't realize there were pickpockets on the subways and buses. Wayne also had no sense of direction, so he easily got lost. There were no GPS devices yet.

He enjoyed country and western music and I liked rock and roll. I loved to travel, and had already been to Europe on a field trip with my grade thirteen class. He had gone to the University of Guelph, which was about an hour and a half from his house, and that was as far as he had travelled. Nevertheless, I loved him and wanted to marry him. In one way, we weren't so different—we had been brought up with the same moral and ethical values.

We got engaged in 1976 on Valentine's Day, and were married in May 1977. It was a beautiful sunny day with no wind, fortunately, as we had our pictures done at Canatara Park, which is right on Lake Huron.

The sandy beach stretches for miles. It has many big, beautiful trees that add a magnificent backdrop for pictures.

All my relatives came from Toronto. We really had a great time. Since my dad had already died, my brother gave me away. My dad's brother, Uncle Calvin, was the master of ceremonies since he was my favourite uncle. Our honeymoon was a camping trip to the east coast of Canada. The scenery there was beautiful, and it was a nice break after all the planning we had done for the wedding.

We had a wonderful time, celebrating the beginning of our life together. After such a strong start, I was sure our marriage would be nothing but bliss.

Wayne hurries into the waiting room with steaming coffee.

"Any news?" he asks.

No, I shake my head.

I'm feeling stressed as the hours tick by slowly. I flash back to happier events to try and stay calm while I sip my delicious coffee

Chapter Four

Wayne's Family Life

We visited Wayne's parents' farm often. Wayne's mom, Mary, would always be in the kitchen baking cookies, preparing supper, or doing some sewing. She made a quilt by hand every winter. I was amazed, having never seen anyone hand-quilt on a big frame. I acquired my love of quilting from Mary, and have made many beautiful quilts over the years. We were fortunate to receive a large Colonial Lady quilt from her as a wedding present. Her baking was incredible too, especially her butter tarts and rhubarb pie. I loved to bake as well, and was very interested in her recipes so I could try to be a great baker just like her. Each time we would visit the farm, I enjoyed touring all the beautiful flower gardens with Mary.

Wayne's dad was nicknamed Jiggs, although his real name was Emerson. He was proud of his vegetable garden, where he grew beans, tomatoes, carrots, corn, potatoes, and cucumbers. My favourite memory was seeing the pumpkins getting bigger, because my dad and I had grown them in Toronto when I was a child. Jiggs was always busy on the farm, fixing things like broken fence posts and tractors, or cleaning out the barns. One time, he took us into the milk barn and showed us how to milk the cows, and then we got to taste the milk right out of the big storage tank. That was exciting, but I didn't like how dirty the barn was—and it smelled bad, too.

One winter, Jiggs took us for a horse-drawn sleigh ride in an old-fashioned cutter. The cutter had steel runners like skis, so it went through the snow like butter. We were all wrapped up in blankets. The sun shone on our faces and the sky was blue, but it was freezing, with a strong north wind. It was a ride I'll never forget.

Wayne grew up in a loving and caring family atmosphere. When he arrived home from school on his bike, his senses would be filled with the smells of supper in the oven, homemade pies, cakes, and always cookies. He came from a Christian family that gave thanks to God before every meal. A lot of joking went on between the brothers and sister at mealtimes. Homemade quilts decorated every bed and kept the family warm. The freezer was full of meat from the beef cattle they raised, the fridge had milk from their dairy cows, and their chickens provided eggs and meat. Wayne's mom would pluck out the feathers to get them ready for the pot. Wayne would tell me stories of chickens running around the yard with their heads cut off. It was barbaric, I thought, but that was how they killed them. A few pigs supplied bacon and pork chops. There was always a cat with kittens in the hayloft in the barn. The garden had a good harvest every fall, and I always looked forward to the meals from the garden.

When I think of it, they had everything they needed—a loving family and food in their bellies. I wanted that for my family, too, so years later, when we had children, I took them to the farm as often as I could, hoping it would rub off on us. This happiness was a gift I could give my family.

CHAPTER FIVE

My Family Life Growing up in Toronto

My mom and dad met in Scotland during the Second World War. When I asked how they met, my mother told me that all the enlisted girls would take the train into the city for dances with other soldiers. My mom was in the air force and my dad was in the army. Mom met my dad at the dance several times, and was attracted to him and his Canadian accent.

One night as he was leaving to go back on the train to his barracks, he yelled out the window, "Evelyan, will you marry me?" Of course she said yes. She was only twenty years old—the youngest of fourteen children born into a good Irish-Catholic home. My parents were married in a small civil service in April of 1944. My dad continued to fight for the Fort Garry Regiment, and was sent to France on June 6, 1944 as part of the Normandy invasion. He landed on Juno beach in a amphibious Sherman tank transported by a Navy ship.

My mom stayed near Stranraer, Scotland in the women's air force, where she lived in the barracks with the other women. When the war ended in 1945, she moved back to Glasgow and shared a bedroom with her sister Lily until my dad could save enough money to send for her. She was eager to get out of her sister's bedroom at home and move to Canada.

My mother came alone on the Queen Mary II, the world's biggest ocean liner at the time. I have a small brooch depicting the ship that she was given when she boarded. It is very special to me because it reminds me of the start of her life with my dad. She had to have been very determined and gutsy to leave everything she knew and come to a strange country! On the ship, she knew no one and wondered if she had done the right thing by leaving her friends and family thousands of miles away. The ship was at sea for two weeks before docking in Halifax. My goal is to one day visit Pier 21, where she disembarked.

My mother took a train from Halifax to Toronto, where my dad met her at Union Station. Although Dad was born in Saskatchewan, he had moved to Toronto with his parents and ten brothers and sisters in 1936, when he was about sixteen years old.

When my parents bought a home in Scarborough, they planted a big garden in the backyard. My dad worked at the veterans' hospital in the day and as a bartender at night so that my mother wouldn't have to work. In those days, women were to stay home with the children and tend the house. My brother, Garry, was born in May 1947. They named him after the Fort Garry Regiment in Winnipeg where my dad had been stationed during the war.

My dad loved children and wanted a whole houseful. My mom didn't really want any more, but she told me that she got pregnant with me when her diaphragm broke. When she told me this, I felt unwanted. After all, didn't Catholics like my mother believe children were a blessing? Personally, I wanted a large family and I couldn't imagine ever telling any of my children that they weren't wanted. I looked forward to every child that would come along.

I was born in May 1952. During the cold winter nights at home in Toronto when I was growing up, my mom taught me how to embroider and knit. She never got frustrated when I dropped stitches during the knitting lessons; she just fixed it for me. We often played board games or cards. Sunday dinner was always a rump roast with mashed potatoes and corn that we ate off of our "good dishes," which we had obtained by buying boxes of laundry detergent—a promotion at the time. My mom would spend all day making pastry for the apple pie, which she served with vanilla ice cream. I always looked forward to all of us sitting down on Sundays since it was the only time we were all together at a meal. My dad worked nights, including Saturdays, so we only had Sunday together. We would always go out for a walk in the afternoon with our Labrador retriever, Champ. Somehow we always ended up at the corner store to get a treat.

I was the only one in our family to go to church. I also joined a girls' group at the church called Canadian Girls in Training, or C.G.I.T. I remember making bandages for cancer patients. We studied the Bible and played games. A highlight of my summer was going to our leader's cottage for the weekend—we'd go for walks and go out in the canoe. Our core group still meets once a year at the leader's house for a reunion. She is ninety-two now.

I had a part-time job at the Dominion store as a cashier during my high school years. I was the only one on both sides of the family to go to university. I took Secretarial Studies, which included law, and French was my minor. My parents were proud when I graduated.

My dad had cardiac problems from a young age, and when he was forty-seven years old he had a heart attack. He changed his diet and was able to live seven more years before a fatal heart attack took his life. He and my mom had been married for thirty-one years.

I was twenty-two at the time of his death, and was working in the south of France as an *au pair* for a family. Actually, I had decided to take some time off work and had left the French family to go travelling. I went all the way up to the tip of Norway, but it was getting cold up there in October, so I decided to go back to France. My brother Garry had been frantically searching for me in Europe through Interpol. I had just returned when the phone rang in my host family's living room. They ran to get me—they didn't speak English, but they understood the word "Sandra." My brother gave me the sad news; I cried most of the night and didn't get much sleep.

I returned to Canada the very next day. I took a small plane to Paris in the morning and I was supposed to connect to another plane to Toronto a few hours later, but unfortunately I missed it. I was alone at the airport and couldn't stop crying. I feared I would miss the funeral, but I managed to get on the next plane, and when I arrived at the airport Wayne and my best friend Judy were waiting for me. I hugged them for what seemed to be an eternity, all the time bawling my eyes out. I couldn't believe this was happening—that my dad was really dead.

Garry and Mom were already at the funeral home. I arrived there at nine that evening to see my dad for the last time. As I gazed on his still face, a flashback to the last time I had seen him alive crossed my mind. It was May 13, 1974—Mother's Day—and he waved to me and blew me a kiss before I entered the security door for my flight to France. How could I have known that it was the last time I would see him?

We buried my dad the morning after I arrived home. I was closer to my dad than my mom, and a piece of me went with him that day.

It's now well into the afternoon, and we're getting hungry. We don't want to leave the waiting room for fear there might be someone coming out to tell us that Darryl hasn't survived. We have no idea how long the operation is going to take—there's a team of transplant surgeons that includes stomach, liver, bladder and kidneys, heart, bowel, pancreas and spleen, as well as all the surgical nurses and anaesthetist. The room must be really big to accommodate all the people and equipment.

At 3:30 p.m., the nurse comes out and again says Darryl is doing fine, but it will be a long time before the doctors are done. As we continue to wait, I begin to reminisce about our first home.

CHAPTER SIX

Our Family Beginnings

I liked Wayne's big family, and thought it would be great to have four children. He liked that idea too. We had both been brought up not to buy anything unless we could pay cash for it. As we had no debts, we started to save for the house we both wanted. We would need a mortgage, but we were determined to make a big down payment and avoid buying anything on credit. Our dreams were coming true.

Wayne and I moved into an apartment while the house we had chosen was being built. Both of us learned how to cook, and we were very happy. We had many decisions to make regarding the new house. We had bought a semi-detached house, meaning that both sides had to have the same exterior brick colour. Fortunately, the neighbour had picked out the same yellow-brown brick colour as us. We meticulously chose floor coverings and kitchen cabinets so everything would match. We moved in on New Year's Eve, because the government would give us a grant if we were in by December 31, 1976.

The builder had painted all the walls white so that we could pick our own colours. Since we were now experienced painters, we chose beige for the walls in the main living area. Our bedroom was sky blue, and the other two bedrooms were yellow and green. I appropriated the sunny yellow room for my sewing room, where I made all the drapes for the house. Harvest-gold appliances complemented the dark brown cabinets in the kitchen. We bought an inexpensive couch and chair that soon became worn and torn, teaching us the importance of buying good furniture that would last and wouldn't need to be constantly replaced. As a result, we saved up and bought a real wood dining room set that we use to this day—and it still looks beautiful. For birthdays and Christmas, people gave us things for the house. My mom offered us tea towels, pots and pans, utensils, and old bath towels, and I accepted everything. Wayne's mom gave us tulip bulbs and a rose bush for Mother's Day.

As relatives died and we received inheritance money, we applied it to our mortgage so we wouldn't have to pay as much interest on the house. I was gradually coming to love antiques, since most the stuff we had was old.

Wayne built me a long clothesline in the backyard with a pulley system so I could hang out my wash like our mothers had done all their lives. I was astonished that some of my friends lived in communities that did not allow clotheslines. The clothes smelled so clean when I brought them inside, and they had been brightened by the sun. Planning ahead for any children we might have, we fenced in the yard. Wayne built a shed for the lawnmower and garden tools.

We didn't have much furniture, and really no money, so a lot of the rooms sat empty for a long time. One day, the paper boy came to collect his money. As he stood in the foyer, he asked us, "Why doesn't anyone on this street have furniture in the living room?" We laughed. Everyone on the street was young like we were, and they didn't have any extra money either.

I wanted to pay down the mortgage as fast as we could, and purchase some furniture for the living room, so I made all our meals from scratch because it was cheaper and more wholesome. We had lots of examples of thriftiness to follow. Wayne's mom preserved or pickled vegetables from the garden, including cucumbers and beets. She also made homemade relish and pies, and sewed beautiful quilts, and I wanted to be just like her. Wayne's Aunt Edna always sewed each niece a nightgown for Christmas on her old sewing machine. Even into her eighties, she made about thirty-five nightgowns every Christmas. She always chose the right size for each child even though she never had any children of her own. She was amazing.

Florence, the mother of our sister-in-law Alice (who was married to Wayne's brother Don), made the best buns. I went to her farm one Saturday to learn how she did it. Florence told me to measure five or six cups of flour with a broken tea cup, not a measuring cup. Since I didn't have a broken tea cup, she sent me home with buns and a cup with a broken handle so I could make my own. Unfortunately, my buns were never as good as Florence's, so we always let Alice make them for special occasions, since she had inherited the knack for making delicious buns.

Once when they were younger, Wayne and his friends were at Alice's house playing cards with her brother Jeff. Florence had made a large batch of delicious-looking buns, then went to the church to get things ready for Sunday school. When she returned, all the buns had been eaten. She was so mad at the boys. Wayne has never forgotten that night, or how good those buns tasted.

Wayne and I put in a large garden, and I began canning all sorts of vegetables and fruits such as strawberries and blueberries. In addition, we picked apples and peaches from the trees in our backyard, and stored everything that hadn't been canned in our giant chest freezer. I made homemade spaghetti sauce from our tomatoes, as well as chili sauce. Pastry was an art that I mastered, and our freezer was full of cherry and apples pies. I followed the cranberry sauce recipe passed down from my paternal grandma, who had grown up in Saskatchewan, and we had that every Thanksgiving, along with pumpkin pie made from fresh pumpkins. We were blessed with lots of food for the family, and I was trying to be the best wife ever by feeding my husband and keeping a clean home. Our life together was full, and very happy. We had every reason to believe that we were fully prepared for whatever might come our way next.

CHAPTER SEVEN

The Calm Before the Storm

We had two mortgages, because one credit union could only give us twenty-five thousand dollars. That was our first mortgage, and we amortized it over twenty-five years to make the payments smaller. We had to go to another credit union to get the remaining twelve thousand dollars, which was considered a second mortgage. Three years later, we had almost paid off that second mortgage, and we decided to start a family.

I worked as a secretary in the latex division of Polysar during the day, and sold Tupperware at night. Wayne would often come home to a living room full of product that I was bagging for customers. The phone rang day and night with people wanting to buy Tupperware for their homes. I was extremely busy working my day job at Polysar, and every night I was out doing Tupperware parties. I met so many people, some of whom are still my closest friends today. I got to know the streets of Sarnia, and even some county roads. It was scary to drive in the country alone at night, but I found that the country folk were very friendly. They loved to have parties so they could get together. I was doing so well in my home business that I was promoted to manager.

A double brick wall with a twelve-inch space between the bricks separated our semi-detached house from the other half. Sometimes you could hear the next-door neighbour having a shower, but other than that it was quiet. All the people on our street were young, and most of them had children already

My dream was always to have a house of my own with lots of children. When I became pregnant, I was so excited to get our child's room ready. Of course, we didn't know if it was a girl or boy. We painted the room yellow, and I also made bumper pads that were yellow and bought yellow sheets. My Tupperware teammates, the "Livewires," threw me a shower. One of the ladies in my group came over and cleaned the house for me, which I appreciated very much. To be on the safe side, everyone gave us yellow baby outfits at the shower.

Knowing that I wanted a pediatrician for our children, I began thinking about who I would go to and who was taking patients. Little did I realize that the one I found would be an invaluable resource and fantastic doctor not only for my first baby, but also for the children we were to have in the future.

We were ready.

CHAPTER EIGHT

Our First-Born, Leanne

Leanne was born on a sunny day in July 1978. Her colouring was very different than Wayne's and mine. We had brown hair and brown eyes, while she had blue eyes and blonde hair. All the yellow outfits I had received at the shower looked nice on her. Unfortunately, we had gone camping just before Leanne was born, and I had come into contact with poison ivy. The nurses wrapped Saran Wrap over the rash on my arms so that I could hold her and nurse her in the hospital.

Leanne had colic and cried a lot the first three months. Our perfect world started to fray around the edges. My mom came from Toronto for two weeks to help me—she cooked the meals and cleaned the house as if it were the queen's residence. It was so nice to go to bed with sheets that had been hung on the line. They smelled so fresh and clean. Leanne tended to spit up a lot, so there was always laundry to do. I missed my mom when she went home.

When Leanne started eating solids at six months of age, I made all her baby food myself. I froze it in ice cube trays so it could be heated up quickly. There were no microwaves then, so I heated it up in little dishes in pots of water. I bought a yogurt maker and fed her homemade yogurt every day so that she would have natural bacteria to fight off infection. I recorded every milestone in her baby book with lots of pictures. I kept my house clean and tidy. In short, I was trying to be supermom.

I belonged to a support group for women who were nursing babies. Some women were extreme and nursed their kids for years. I decided that nursing Leanne for one year would be enough to give her a healthy start and a strong immune system to cope with childhood germs.

The first camping trip we went on after Leanne was born was to Pinery Provincial Park, which was only an hour from home. Our best friends, whose son was a month older than Leanne, went with us. Leanne was two months old. She slept in a playpen in our small, three-person tent. In the daytime, we would move the playpen outside and she would sleep in the fresh air. We took Leanne for many walks in the stroller that my Aunt Lily had bought me when my mom and I visited her in Scotland the year before. Aunt Lily was the older sister my mom had lived with while waiting to come to Canada to join my father after the war.

I had always wanted to camp in Algonquin Park, so we made the seven-hour trip there for our holidays the following year. We camped near the water so Leanne could play in the sand at the beach. We also took a trip out west to visit Aunt Kitty, my dad's older sister, in Calgary. It was a long, hot trip, but we had fun.

One day we went to Dinosaur Provincial Park, near Drumheller, Alberta, where all the dinosaur bones are. The on-site museum featured displays recounting the history of the area, as well as skeletons and pictures of dinosaurs. While there, we climbed all over the hills in the badlands. Leanne enjoyed getting out of her car seat and running around. It was a great day.

As a child, Leanne had fun riding her tricycle. One day when her nana—my mom—was babysitting, Leanne got her toe stuck in the spokes and lost her big toenail. My mom cannot stand the sight of blood or vomit. She almost gets sick herself. Unfortunately, I was still at work. My mom didn't drive, so she had to deal with it then and there. She knew enough to apply pressure and put ice on the big toe until the blood stopped oozing out. When I returned home at suppertime, she told me how frightened she had been to see all the blood. She said Leanne was screaming, but after the initial shock she was quite brave about it and calmed down.

Our daughter always wanted to be independent and would try to do things for herself like pouring her own juice. One time while she was doing so, Leanne dropped a forty-eight ounce can of juice on her other big toe. That time the nail turned black, but it stayed on. She cried a lot, which made me feel horrible.

Like most parents, we were likely over-cautious with our first child. Or maybe we weren't always cautious enough, as she once fell out of the top bunk bed and broke her front tooth.

Grandpa and Grandma really enjoyed having Leanne for the weekend. During the summer, Leanne spent quite a few weekends at the farm. She started playing soccer when she was four years old, and was a very good player. Every summer she took swimming lessons as well. My mom was afraid of the water and couldn't swim—my mother's mom had drowned when my mom was three years old, so her fear was understandable. Still, I didn't want any of my children to be afraid of the water.

Grandpa would play "peekaboo" with Leanne. She never stopped giggling as he peeked around a corner. She even laughed when he just put his hands up in front of his eyes. He would take her to the barn every morning when he was going to milk the cows. She found it very interesting that the milk she drank for breakfast came out of those cows. She loved playing with the kittens in the barn as well. She wanted to stay at the farm and live there instead of coming back home.

Leanne took a big yellow school bus all the way across the city to Lake Road Public School. She enjoyed school, but it was tiring and she often fell asleep on the bus on the way home. Still, it was a nice change for me to have a few hours to myself again.

We always did our best to keep her safe. However, as we were about to find out, sometimes even when parents do everything possible to protect their children, bad things happen to them anyway.

Now that we know we won't hear anything soon about Darryl, we decide to go to the cafeteria downstairs in the hospital to get some food. It's 5 p.m., and there aren't many people left in the surgical waiting room. We hurry downstairs and bring our food back with us just in case. As we eat, I begin thinking about our second-born, Heather, and all the medical issues we've experienced with her.

CHAPTER NINE

Our Second Child, Heather

I went back to work at Polysar, now called Nova Chemical, as a part-time secretary when Leanne was one. When she was almost two, I became pregnant with our next child. I was bleeding so much that I had to stop work. The doctor said I had placenta previa: the placenta was covering the cervix, so if I lifted something heavy or worked too hard around the house, I would bleed.

I had to rest a lot, which was hard to do with a child in the house. I had to stop selling Tupperware. Wayne was happy about that, because by now the basement was full of unsold product. I also had to stop working at Polysar.

When Leanne was two-and-a-half years old, Heather was born on a snowy Sunday morning in December. The doctor laid her on my stomach, and a strange look crossed his face.

My chest tightened. "What is it?"

He examined her in silence for several minutes, then pulled a chair to the side of the bed and sat down. "Your daughter has a myelomeningocele, or—in plain terms—spina bifida, which is a hole in her lower spine."

I stared down at the tiny little one in my arms and my stomach lurched. Blood vessels and bone were visible, because the skin was all pulled back on either side of her spine.

While she lay crying on my chest, the doctor calmly said to the nurse, "Put a sterile four by four gauze on it." Our doctor was from Scotland and he said the disability was more common over there. He said that children with spina bifida often had trouble with their bowel and bladder, but usually had a long life.

I had just watched a show on television in October about children with spina bifida from the United Kingdom. The program outlined some of the physical and mental challenges a child with spina bifida would possibly face. I'd felt sorry for the parents who had to do all this extra work to keep their child alive, and remembered thinking, *Surely in this day and age this disease can be prevented.* Before the show, I had no idea what spina bifida was. Looking back, I believe God was preparing me for the birth of Heather. It was too much of a coincidence.

I'd had an ultrasound while I was pregnant, and it had shown a normal-sized baby—and indeed, Heather weighed eight pounds, nine ounces when she was born. She had lots of dark brown hair. There were no special needs children in either Wayne's family or mine. Wayne's mom told us that her two sisters had died at seven and nine months of age, but she didn't know what they had died from. In the early 1900s, there were no autopsies done in their rural area. I had eaten well during the pregnancy, I never smoked or drank alcohol, and I took prenatal vitamins. I couldn't believe I had given birth to a special needs child. But from the beginning, Wayne was always optimistic that she would survive and do well.

I was very glad we already had a great pediatrician who would expertly look after Heather when we got home. That wouldn't be able to happen for a while, though. Our daughter was taken immediately to Victoria Hospital in London, Ontario, a larger city an hour east of Sarnia, where she would remain for a few months. I had to stay in Sarnia for about a week until I could travel. I remember praying, "Please God, let her live." I was afraid she would die before I got to see her again.

Wayne drove down to London behind the ambulance to make sure our little girl was well taken care of. His mom met him at the hospital, and they both cried. Wayne's mom couldn't believe that her sweet, easygoing son had a disabled child. Wayne drove to London every day after work to check on Heather, then he would come and see me in Sarnia to let me know how she was.

When I was released from the hospital, I went straight to London to nurse Heather. I had been pumping my milk and storing it in the freezer all week. Wayne's mom came to Sarnia to look after Leanne. It was difficult for me to be in London with Heather while Leanne and Wayne were back in Sarnia, even though Wayne faithfully visited on Wednesdays and Saturdays.

On top of the emotional turmoil, I was exhausted. I couldn't sleep well on the cot in Heather's room because the nurses came in with a flashlight every hour during the night to check on her. In spite of the hardships, though, I had to be with my daughter. I needed to know that she was getting the best possible treatment, and I wanted to learn how to take care of her when we got home.

Heather had a good neurosurgeon. He had to operate within twenty-four hours to close her back before infection entered her spine. It was mind-boggling how many doctors were involved in caring for her. I had never studied anything about the human body, so I was learning a lot of medical terms.

Heather had to have a lot of tests. One was to determine if the fluid was collecting in her brain instead of draining down her spine like it normally would. They found that the pressure in the ventricles in her brain was higher than normal, so the neurosurgeon decided to put a shunt in. The shunt was a little pump that kept the cerebral fluid from pooling in her brain, a condition called hydrocephalus. A long tube was attached to the pump so the fluid would travel down the tubing and into her abdomen instead of down her defective spine. This tube would need to be lengthened as she grew.

When I first saw Heather after her surgery, I was surprised to see staples in her head. Clear fluid oozed out of the holes around the staples. The doctor assured me this was normal, and we just had to keep the incision clean so infection would not get into her brain. Her stomach was also closed with staples where the tube from her brain had been routed through her neck and then into the abdomen. Stapling incisions instead of using stitches was a new procedure in the 1980s, and it looked painful. The nurses taught Wayne and me how to clean and dress our daughter's incisions with a topical antiseptic and sterile gauze.

When Heather was two months old, Wayne and I met with the geneticist in London. "Your daughter will probably not walk and will need to be in a wheelchair all her life. Her math and language skills will be delayed due to the placement of her shunt," he said with authority. I felt he must know what he was talking about since he was about fifty years old and had a lot of experience.

I asked, "If Heather was your daughter, what interventions would you do?"

I was horrified when he replied, "I wouldn't do anything." Without closing her back or putting in a shunt to drain the fluid from her head, she would have died. I think he said that because he knew how difficult a struggle Heather would have just to survive. He also knew how much work it would be for us to take care of her.

Wayne and I didn't agree with the geneticist. We were both determined to do everything possible so that Heather could have a fighting chance at a normal life. We also wanted to know what the likelihood was that any future children we might have would face the same disability. "What are the chances we could have another spina bifida child?" I asked.

"The risk is low—about one in 250," he stated.

Another child with the same condition had been born the day before Heather at the same hospital in Sarnia. As it turned out, that fall more babies were born with spina bifida in the Windsor-Sarnia corridor than in any other part of Canada. Spina bifida is a polygenetic disability, which means that something in the environment—in the water or the air (we live in chemical valley)—plus a genetic factor in both my husband and me, combined to produce a child with spina bifida. The condition is also more prevalent in people with an Irish, Scottish, or Welsh background. My mom was born in Ireland, Wayne's mom had Welsh ancestors, and his dad had Scottish in his background.

After a few weeks of helping us take care of Leanne, Wayne's mom had to go back home to the farm to look after Jiggs. Thankfully, my mother was able to come stay at our house until I was finally able to return home with our little girl two months later. I hardly recognized my own house.

I made an appointment with our knowledgeable pediatrician as soon as I got home. I felt confident he would be a key player in her development.

At six months of age, Heather was referred to a pediatric ophthalmologist because she had strabismus in her eyes when she was born. Her eyes turned outward due to a muscle imbalance. She had trouble focussing, and her hand-eye coordination was not very good. Heather had an operation in London at nine months of age where the pediatric ophthalmologist tightened the muscles in her eyes so that they were oriented straight. With every challenge there always seemed to be a solution, though the surgeries were stressful every time.

I was given a poem written by Anna Marie Jaworski entitled "Eleven Things I Wish my Child's Doctor Knew," which sums up the way I felt.

1. Please don't ask me to leave my child's side. I can't eat or rest knowing something could happen while my child is outside the safety of my arms. I need to be there.

2. I need to be part of my child's care team. I am there everyday. I am used to being in charge. At home, no nurses or doctors are there telling me what to do. Help me be a better part of the team.

3. I am not stupid. I may not understand the words you use, but I am willing to learn. Teach me. Help me understand what you're talking about. What could be more important for me to know?

4. I am not overprotective. I am a parent. I have seen my child struggle to survive. God gave me this child to protect and to love. If I am doing something excessive, then kindly, gently tell me it's not necessary. But do not tell me I am overprotective—those words are fighting words.

5. I don't know if you believe in God or not, but I hope you do. While my child is under the care of your hands, I am in the waiting room asking for God to guide your hands and your mind so you can save my child. I pray for you.

6. Caring for a child with a chronic illness isn't what I bargained for when planning my family. This is the hardest thing I've ever had to deal with. I am not just my child's parent; I have many roles and wear many hats. Please understand this problem has touched every facet of my life and is challenging me in ways you cannot see.

7. I am grieving. This is NOT what I planned. My home is waiting for my child. Clothes hang in the closets; toys and books are waiting to serve their purposes. Please be kind while I try to grasp what all of this means and while I mourn the life my child should have had.

8. I trust you. I have handed over the most important, most helpless person in my life. I know you aren't God, but I am hoping that through you God can work a miracle.

9. I have hope. I don't care about statistics. There aren't 100 of my children here at the same time having the same operation. There is one and that child is mine. Don't tell me that you don't think my child will make it. Tell me that you'll do everything in your power to help my child survive.

10. I know you don't have a crystal ball. When I ask you for my child's prognosis, I am asking for reassurance. Every parent wants to know they'll be a grandparent someday. Don't get irritated when I ask about the future. Tell me I'm doing a good job today.

11. If it is God's will to take my child too soon, don't be afraid to let me see you cry. Your tears will help to cleanse my wounded heart. I need to know you cared.

CHAPTER TEN

Heather's Challenges

I was determined that Heather would be just like every other child. I ate, breathed, and slept spina bifida. I researched everything I could find using books from the library. We didn't have the internet in those days, but the London Hospital had a very good medical library I could use when Heather was asleep (I didn't leave her side when she was awake).

When we got home, our pediatrician referred us to the Rotary Children's Place, a centre for children with developmental and physical problems. They had computers we could use to look up things online. An Easter Seals nurse also came to the house to assess Heather's needs as far as medical equipment was concerned, and to help with funding for her other medical needs.

The neatest thing was Heather learning to swim at the YMCA, where she had a special swim instructor from the Rotary Children's Place. At two months of age, Heather was skillfully pushed underwater by Pam, the instructor, toward my open arms a few feet way. We blew in Heather's face before we pushed her under the water. It was amazing to see Heather automatically hold her breath and open her big brown eyes as she flailed her arms and legs, trying to move toward me.

I wanted Heather to be able to crawl, sit, and walk just like any other child. I had no idea that the lack of muscle tone would make this challenging for her. She would cry all the time during her physiotherapy sessions (that started around two months, like her swimming lessons), and I wondered if I was doing the right thing. It was hard for me to watch. Would it be better to do physiotherapy when she got older, rather than when she was a baby? The physiotherapist at the Rotary Children's Place assured me that when kids got older, they refused to do anything, so we had to persevere now.

She had physiotherapy and occupational therapy a few times a week, as well as doctor's visits to specialists in London—a urologist, neurologist, ophthalmologist, psychologist, physiotherapist, occupational therapist, and a bowel and bladder nurse. It was exhausting. I felt overwhelmed and incompetent. In addition, she had a pediatrician in Sarnia and clinic visits with other doctors at the Rotary Children's Place.

Heather had no control of her bowel and bladder and had to be catheterized every four hours. That involved inserting a long plastic tube through her urethra into her bladder. If this wasn't done, urine would just sit in her bladder and cause a urinary infection. A special nurse taught us how to do this procedure. She explained that Heather would eventually learn to catheterize herself, but I didn't believe her. It was hard enough for me to catheterize Heather, and I could see what I was doing! Heather would have to do it by feel.

Further, our little girl had to have enemas every few days to make sure the stool didn't press on the shunt tubing in her abdomen, blocking it. She also had trouble with dexterity and had a hard time picking things up off the floor. My hopes of her being like any other child were falling apart. Even though I'd taken prenatal vitamins and lots of folic acid, eaten right, and exercised, those things hadn't prevented me from having a special needs child.

When we attended clinics at the Thames Valley Children's Centre in London, we saw many other children with spina bifida. Every time I saw a child younger than Heather with the disease, I thought, *Why can't they prevent this disability?* If they knew it could be prevented by taking a certain amount of folic acid, why were babies still being born with spina bifida? The truth is that folic acid reduces the number of babies with spina bifida, but due to other factors—genetics and environmental issues—children with spina bifida are still being born as I write this book.

At seven months of age, the doctor in London explained that Heather would need a special brace so she could sit up like other children her age. I understood this, because due to her lack of muscle tone, if we propped Heather up on the couch she would just fold in half with her head touching her toes.

I remember going to a support group for women breastfeeding their babies that night with Heather, and I met my best friend there with her baby boy.

"How did the visit go today with the doctor?" my friend asked.

I started to cry, because I didn't want Heather to have any special equipment that would mark her as being different from other children.

After I explained what had happened, my friend said she was sorry and hoped the brace would only be temporary. She prayed with me and I felt like I could cope again, knowing that God was watching over us.

The doctor at the clinic had said that Heather would probably never walk. I was determined that she would walk and I expressed this to my friend with real determination.

At the Rotary Children's Place, we had a scooter made that Heather could sit in. It had a long handle, like a wagon, so we could pull her around the room in order for her to get a sense of movement. Her brace fit right into the scooter and helped her to sit up straight.

I devised ways to entice her to accomplish little tasks. For example, when Heather wanted something, I would put it just out of her reach so she would have to figure out how to get it. When Heather was one, she wasn't strong enough to get up on all fours, but she learned to crawl by using her arms and pulling herself along the floor. The physiotherapist called it commando crawling, like soldiers do in the dirt. I saw other children crawling this way, so I thought it was alright.

I put cheese on a plate at the end of the kitchen floor to give her the incentive to crawl to it. I kept moving the cheese farther away until she learned she could get other things too—like toys. It worked, and after a lot of effort, she crawled everywhere. In order to make her roll over, I held up a toy just to the right of her eyes while she was on her stomach. When she looked up, she automatically rolled over. I would also have to physically roll her over daily, first one way and then the other way, so she got used to the feeling.

We were a little afraid to take Heather camping, but when we got the all clear from the doctors that her back, stomach, and head had healed, we headed to Algonquin Park in the summer with our tent. Heather was six months old and Leanne was three. Heather got to sleep in the playpen this time. She loved hearing the Berenstain Bears stories at bedtime because we had told her there were bears in the woods.

On our camping trip, we took the girls out in the canoe. Heather loved the motion, but we did a stupid thing. We couldn't figure out how she would sit up in the canoe, so we strapped her into her carseat and set it in the middle of the canoe. If Heather had fallen out, she would have gone right to the bottom of the lake before we could get to her.

Fortunately, she didn't fall out. Unfortunately, we were so busy watching Heather that we didn't see *Leanne* fall out of the canoe at the back end. Leanne always loved bugs and was reaching into the water for one when she toppled overboard. Thankfully, she had her lifejacket on and it had a loop on the headrest, so as we paddled by, we simply scooped her back up into the canoe. She was fine—just a little surprised and crying.

When Leanne was a little older, we practiced tipping the canoe and getting back in so it became a game. We went to a safety canoe demonstration where we learned how to do a canoe over canoe rescue, as well as getting back into a tipped canoe.

One day my best friend came over with her little boy. Our first-born children were a month apart, and our second children were three months apart. She put her son down on the floor. He was about nine months old, and promptly started to crawl away. Heather, who was almost a year old, just lay there on the carpet and watched him. At that moment I felt the pain of my daughter being developmentally delayed. The doctors had been saying those words to me for months, but it hit home when I realized my friend's son was younger and his skills were more developed. I had been so wrapped up in daily therapy that I hadn't had time to get together with my friends and their children to see how they were developing.

I was happy for my friend's baby, but it was hard to watch a younger child do things I knew Heather wasn't able to. Every night I would go to bed wondering if I had done enough for the children, and every night I was exhausted after trying to make it through the day. I had trouble coping and would often just sit and cry.

About this same time, Heather began to attend Lambton College in the infant toddler room. I felt she needed to be with other children her own age. It was a bit unnerving because I wondered if the staff knew what signs to watch for with Heather's shunt if it got blocked. So I wrote down all the information and they included it in Heather's file, which made me feel better.

At two and a half, she graduated to the daycare section for older children up to four years of age. She also started the preschool programs on alternate days at the Rotary Children's Place. Sometimes Heather would have her physio, occupational, and speech therapies at the Rotary Children's Place while she was attending the preschool program. She loved the other children there, and the two hours she spent at daycare gave me a much-needed break, especially since Leanne also went to the college daycare centre at the same time. The Rotary School had a bus that would pick Heather up and bring her home. Therapy and school were exhausting for Heather, and most days she would be asleep on the bus coming home.

A standing brace was made by the Rotary Children's Place when Heather was two. It was a steel frame with straps that fit around her waist and legs. I couldn't imagine how she would ever walk in this brace—and all the other children her age were walking by now.

Ankle foot orthotics (AFOs) were made by Custom Orthotics in London. They took a cast of her feet, and then a plastic mould was made from the cast that had straps on it to fasten to her legs. The AFOs fit into her shoes to give her stability. In order to strengthen her weak leg muscles, she had to stand up for long periods of time in the standing brace, which was exhausting. We set out lots of interesting toys, such as coloured blocks, on the table to keep her attention. I couldn't ever leave her alone because she might fall backwards.

When Heather was in occupational therapy at the Rotary Children's Place, the therapist taught her many important life skills. Every game was geared to a specific goal. The well-known "Patty Cake" song taught her how to get her hands and arms to work together. She had low muscle tone on her left side, so she tended to only use one hand. At occupational therapy, they had her pick up Smarties, beans, and rice to develop her fine motor skills. They put Jell-O, spaghetti, and whipped cream in small kiddie pools that the kids could play with in order to enhance their sensory skills.

Heather eventually learned to walk in the brace by shifting her weight from side to side while pushing herself forward. I distinctly remember the day she first walked. We had come home from church and my mom was visiting. We were sitting in the living room and all of a sudden Heather took a few steps toward my mom. We were thrilled! My mom was so proud, and had a smile from ear to ear—she thought she would never see Heather walk. Mom always felt sorry for Heather, and tended to spoil her. It was a good feeling to see Heather progress, albeit slowly.

Heather needed to go to London for assessments and checkups every month. She had to see a urologist, the bowel and bladder nurse, and the neurosurgeon regularly. I had a special calendar to keep track of all the appointments. When I look back at those calendar planners, I wonder how I got through it. Heather had several operations to lengthen her shunt as she grew taller. Since she had trouble with bowel movements, the nurse would give me recipes for natural laxatives, which helped a lot. Leanne often went with us to London, and to pass the time in the car, we would play the game of who could spot the first horse, cow, or goat. We also played the game of who could spot a license plate that wasn't from Ontario. The kids enjoyed these games.

Even though things were progressing, I was having trouble coping. When Heather was about two years old, I had an emotional breakdown. I remember sitting in the chair and being unable to stop crying. I called Wayne at work and he came home to take care of Heather.

Wayne worked long hours to support the family, so I was responsible for the children and all their needs. It was overwhelming. I thought I'd had a mental breakdown, so I went to the doctor the next morning and he put me on Prozac, an anti-depressant that increased the serotonin level in my blood. I felt better within a few days and was able to cope again. I learned years later that I did poorly when sunlight was limited. This common condition is called Seasonal Affective Disorder (SAD). The winter months were the worst since we don't get much sun in Canada between October and March.

One of our friends suggested we go to a family camp up north on John Island just to get away from the daily routine. It was about a thirteen-hour drive. I wasn't sure I could be in the car that long with a two-and-a-half and a five-year-old. My friend suggested we drive halfway and stay over at her friend's house and then do the rest of the trip the next day. We packed the car and off we all went. Wayne drove almost all the way to North Bay while I tried to keep the children happy. My friend had two daughters who were seven and nine, so Leanne had someone to play with.

When we arrived at the camp the following day, everyone was assigned to sleep in bunk houses except for us. Heather was the youngest child at camp, so we were given the fully-equipped house. It was so much easier for us to have all the facilities—a real blessing.

Heather had long eyelashes, big brown eyes, and curly brown ringlets. At family camp, one of the counsellors took a shine to her. He would carry her around and put his face close to her eyes so she would give him butterfly kisses. Everyone was drawn to her because of her beautiful smile. I usually took care of Heather's needs and Wayne looked after Leanne. I had been worried that it would be too much work for me to take care of Heather, but the counsellor carried her everywhere and she loved it. This gave me a much-needed break to enjoy hiking, canoeing, and sailing with our friends.

We all really enjoyed going to the Easter Seals family camp in Komoka until Heather was seven years old. After that, she could go on her own, which she did until she was twenty. Some of the best times at family camp were when the counsellors took all the children to play games and the parents went off in another direction to have fun together. It was comforting being with other parents who knew how difficult it was to have a disabled child to take care of. All our meals were cooked for us at the camp, which was delightful. We didn't even have to make our beds.

Family rituals were important to us. Heather thrived on routine and repetition. It was important to me to have all the extended family together at Easter, Thanksgiving, Christmas, and birthdays. At Easter we would hide little eggs for the kids to find. Heather's were always on the chair so she could find them easily. For Thanksgiving, Wayne cooked a turkey and I made pies and fresh cranberries. We set out the good china in the dining room and invited all the relatives. My mom had started me on an Old Country Rose pattern of china made by Royal Albert when I was seventeen so I would have a full set of dishes by the time I got married. For Christmas, each child got their own handmade stocking, which I made at night when they were asleep. For their birthdays, they each had a party with their friends and got to choose a favourite cake or pie that I would make.

We read to Heather every night. Since her fine motor skills were delayed, we bought heavy cardboard books so she could help turn the pages. She had one book she really loved called *Ten Little Bears*. Each page had a number from one to ten, and the bears did different things on each page.

Heather's verbal skills were also delayed. When she was mad or frustrated, she would just cry instead of trying to explain to me what was wrong. Trying to figure out what she wanted was frustrating for me, too. The occupational therapist told me to always give her a choice. I was supposed to present her with two outfits in the morning and let her choose which one she wanted to wear. However, she had trouble making decisions, and it always took her about ten minutes to choose. Eventually, though, she liked being able to choose what to wear. Heather had to decide between two choices at breakfast as well. At night she got to pick two stories from the bookcase. It always took her a long time, but she loved selecting the books for us to read.

The following summer we wanted to take Heather on hikes while camping, so we ordered a special backpack carrier for older children from Sweden. It had a nice sturdy base and was big enough to hold a three-year-old. It also had two leg supports at the bottom so it could be set down on a picnic table with Heather still in it. Wayne and I took turns carrying her on hiking trips in Algonquin Park.

SHARING THE CARE

One Saturday we decided to take the kids to the beach at Grand Bend, a small town about an hour north of Sarnia. Leanne and Heather were both very young at the time. It was a lovely, sunny day. The sand was warm and fluffy under our feet, and I had bright pink flip flops on. As we walked across the sand, I stepped on a steel rod buried in the sand. It went right through my foot between my big toe and the next toe. I pulled it out immediately.

Feet and hands tend to bleed a lot, and my foot was no exception. I had to go the hospital in Sarnia immediately. My foot really hurt and was covered in dirty sand. My biggest concern was who would take care of my children if I wasn't there—I knew Wayne wouldn't be able to cope alone.

That incident scared me, and I began teaching Wayne more ways to take care of Heather so he'd be able to do it if I wasn't around. In my eyes, Wayne was a superhero. He not only went to work *every* day—only missing a handful of days in forty years at the office—but he took care of the kids when he got home from work. I always felt he got a break when he went to work and left me with the housework and the kids. There was always a lot of laundry to do since we were using cloth diapers. Heather had to be catheterized because she didn't have control of her bladder, which took time too. The children would fight and cry and make messes that I had to clean up. It seemed so much easier for Wayne to just get dressed and leave the house. He could go out to lunch with his friends. Often people would bring donuts to the office. It wasn't until I began to work once all the kids had left the nest that I realized his job was stressful too.

It was always a challenge for me to trust the experts. Heather needed me to be her voice and advocate so that she received the services she needed. After all, I knew Heather better than anyone else. I knew the doctors knew more of the science and had statistics to quote me, but I was dealing with an individual and I wanted Heather to be just like other children. I always wanted to discuss decisions about her care with the doctor rather than just immediately agreeing to do what they advised.

Since Leanne was older, I always compared Heather's development to Leanne's at the same age. I tended to focus on what Heather couldn't do, rather than on what she could do. I had to change my attitude and continually strive for Heather to reach her potential—whatever that might be.

Chapter Eleven

Leanne Goes on Adventures and Heather Goes to School

When Leanne was about seven years old, she was chosen by the Shriners to go to the Tim Horton's camp in Nova Scotia. The Shriners had been involved with our family since Heather was born. They paid for braces and wheelchairs and always included the disabled children at the parties they organized.

I always felt guilty that I had to spend so much time and energy with Heather. Leanne had to fend for herself a lot, and she grew up faster than normal. We were happy when one of the Shriners came to our house with a very big surprise for Leanne. He said the reason they'd picked Leanne to go to camp was because she was sort of left out since I had to do so much work with Heather. He felt it would be a great opportunity for Leanne to meet new people and have fun. Leanne had never been on a plane or away from us, other than with Mary and Jiggs, and it was kind of scary to let her go off with strangers so far away.

The plane was due to land in Toronto at three o'clock in the afternoon. It had been raining all day and it was getting dark, and when three o'clock came and went, I was worried that something had happened to the plane. I'd already had doubts about letting her go with this group of people I had not met before. We found out around seven o'clock that the flight had been delayed. It wasn't until 9:30 p.m. that night that she arrived back safe and sound—and very tired. She'd been gone for ten days. Leanne still says it was the best trip she has ever taken. She came home with a duffel bag and sleeping bag with "Tim Horton's Camp" stamped on it that we still have to this day.

Leanne had never seen the ocean, and she found it breathtaking. She loved how the giant waves crashed against the rocks and sprayed mist on her face as she breathed in the salty air. One day, all the campers got up really early and went down to the ocean to see the sun rise. Leanne thought it was amazing to watch this giant yellow ball rise out of the sea. The tide also fascinated her, and she collected a lot of shells when the tide was out. Back at camp, she painted a pickle jar blue and glued all the shells on the outside to make a pencil holder. It sits on her desk at her house now as a memento of her trip.

Leanne loved to read Nancy Drew mysteries and Sherlock Holmes books. When she was ten years old, she got a paper route in the neighbourhood. She saved all the money she made and bought a metal detector, and spent many hours at the nearby beach looking for treasures.

HEATHER GOES TO SCHOOL

Heather was the only special needs child at Lakeroad School. The other children were curious about why she needed a walker, and asked her a lot of questions. But when she needed assistance doing anything, the other children were right there to help.

In kindergarten, social skills are really important. Most of the kids couldn't keep still, while Heather couldn't really move very well. She used a rollator walker and could only walk small distances. The kids liked her, but she was always by herself at recess watching the others play. She made friends easily though—probably because she usually had a big smile on her face. Although she couldn't do everything they could, Heather was accepted by the other kids. I never questioned that she'd been born for a reason. She had—and has—a contribution to make to society. I believe God makes people in a certain way to teach us things that we wouldn't learn otherwise so we can fulfil His purpose for us.

When Heather went on field trips, I would accompany her. She especially liked going to the pumpkin patch where there were thousands of pumpkins to see. When they took her to the petting farm, she was afraid of the animals, especially the ones that made a lot of noise like the Canada geese and the donkey. She didn't like dogs or cats either. It took me a long time to realize why she didn't like animals—she moved so slowly that she couldn't run away like other children, and so she was afraid of anything bigger than her. To this day, she dislikes clowns and Santa Claus or anyone else dressed in a costume.

In 1985, Heather was one of the first kids with special needs to be integrated into a regular classroom. The washroom had to be adapted to her individual needs. Under this program, all children went to their district school, regardless of their mental or physical health. The other children were learning about the differences between Heather and themselves. I'd call the other kids in her class "normal" and my friends would reply, "What's normal?"

It was important to me that Heather be integrated into the regular classroom, not only for her own sake, but also so the other kids could learn about the challenges Heather—and other people with special needs—faced.

At first, Heather was labelled mentally and physically handicapped. Then the term was changed to disabled, and now the commonly accepted phrase is a person with special needs. Heather is the same person, but the label has changed. I didn't really like it, but she had to have a label that was recognized by the government so we could get money to help with her additional medical costs. Personally, I think labels are bad because they put people in boxes. However, the Easter Seals nurse helped us to fill out all the necessary papers, and eventually Heather received money from the government. She received drug and dental cards, which paid for the many medications she was taking and her dental care.

When Heather was first tested by a psychologist around age five, they said her IQ scores placed her in the retarded range. I hated that word *retarded*. When I was growing up in Toronto, all the kids I knew that were slow mentally went to the school for retards, and I didn't want her labelled that way. The psychologist said Heather had scattered skill levels and was developmentally delayed. These labels enabled Heather to take advantage of a teaching assistant. Her pediatrician also had to fill out forms regarding her assessment.

A panel of specialists went over her assessments and came up with an individualized program for her. The curriculum would be broken down in small segments so that she could learn at her own pace. They set out specific goals for academic, behavioural, and social skills geared to her learning style. They calculated the time she would spend with the teaching assistant and the amount of time she would be with her peers. I knew Heather was so special and unique, and I wanted the best for her. In math class, the teaching assistant used Smarties to teach her how to count. If Heather got the answer right, she got to eat one piece.

I sewed all her pants for school with heavy fabric because the braces on her legs wore out the pants from the store too fast. She had trouble tying laces, so we bought her shoes with Velcro. She couldn't do buttons, so we bought her clothes with zippers. We bought her a little clown that had buttons, zippers, and Velcro on it so she could practice.

Social workers came to the house weekly to talk to me about the challenges of raising a disabled child and how difficult it could be on a marriage. I'm sure they meant well, but most of them weren't married and didn't have any children, let alone one with special needs. They couldn't really understand what it was like to live in our house. For me, these were just more appointments I didn't want or need.

As Heather got older, we bought a special McLaren buggy for long walks. It was larger than a regular stroller, and could hold a six-year-old. Heather looked completely normal, but she couldn't walk. At Halloween, or when we went to the mall or other places where we would be walking, we would take her in the buggy. Often people would come up to her and say, "You're too big to be in that buggy—you should be walking."

People didn't mean any harm, but it hurt our feelings. Heather wanted to walk just like every other child, but couldn't. These comments were frustrating for our whole family, and I didn't know what to say in response. Eventually, I became so tired of explaining why Heather was in the buggy that I just didn't reply. It did give me insight into how I should react in situations where another disabled person was involved. I have learned to observe rather than blurting out the first thing I think of.

Although I did hold my tongue in those situations, I couldn't help but think that rather than criticizing us, it would have been nice if people had just smiled when they saw Heather in the buggy and asked, "Hello, what's your name, cutie?"

I have always said that Heather taught me patience. I was always in a hurry before she was born. I wanted everything to be done today. But when Heather came along, nothing happened fast. This forced me to slow down and take my time. I could no longer get everything done in one day. Things in the house had to be left until I had enough energy to do them. I came to know which things were important and which things didn't really matter. Heather's development was the most important thing to me.

Chapter Twelve

Heather Grows Older

Heather loved to cook and bake, and we often made cookies, muffins, and chocolates. When we made chocolates for Easter, she used a small paint brush to move the chocolate around in the corners of the mould. She learned how to measure accurately and to stir while holding a spoon with both hands. She liked using the fancy cookie cutters to make different shapes at Christmastime, and then decorating them with coloured sugar and sprinkles. Not only were these activities fun for Heather, they also developed her fine motor skills.

Heather learned to use the phone at the life skills program at the Rotary Children's Place. Eventually she was able to sign her name. The teachers at her school said that she really didn't need to learn this because the world was changing over to computers, but I thought it was a good skill to have, because all legal documents had to be signed. These were life skills that Heather would need to succeed. She continued to struggle with reading and grammar, however, and we didn't think she could cope in the French class, so she was exempted.

At the Rotary Children's Place, the parents formed a group so we could lobby the government to get more services for our children. The meetings were good, because I could relate to the other parents who were going through the same things we were. We shared ideas to help each other with everyday living, and had bake and craft sales to raise money for equipment. I was Heather's advocate to get the services and equipment she needed in order to be able to survive in the world. I knew I couldn't prepare her for everything she was going to have to go through, but I needed to try.

Heather was chosen to be the "Easter Seal Tammy" when she was nine years old. One year the Easter Seal Society chose a disabled girl and the next year they chose a disabled boy to represent all the disabled children in Ontario. She attended many functions with the Easter Seals and Rotarians. She had her picture taken with a Shriner that appeared in the Shrine Circus Magazine that year. She was very proud to be honoured with the privilege. Every June, the Shrine Circus would come to the Sarnia Arena for a few days. We always looked forward to getting free front row seats for the whole family. It was so exciting to see the tigers and elephants and the people on the trapeze!

Heather learned to read books in Grade Five. We were very proud of that achievement. Math continued to be difficult for her, though. Her program had been modified so that she could achieve her goals.

Heather had her ankle straightened at the Shriner's Hospital in Montreal when she was around twelve. Heather went to the school there at the hospital, where she learned how to space her words as she printed. They taught her to place her index finger between the last word and the new one. On Fridays, the patients also learned to cook and bake at the Shriner's kitchen school. Heather loved Fridays the most, because not only did they bake but they got to eat it afterwards. She also had a great teacher and a teaching assistant who spent a lot of time with her.

When she was in Grade Six, we transferred her to the separate Catholic school board because I felt they had a better program for disabled children. She thrived there. It was a proud moment to see her graduate from Grade Eight with her peers after passing with flying colours. She was so happy.

As she grew older, we realized that one of Heather's strengths was her fantastic memory. No one needed a list when they went out shopping with her because she remembered every place we had to go and all the items we needed to buy. She has a photographic memory, which is a real strength.

However, if you asked Heather to do the dishes, she would always leave a few in the sink, and when she vacuumed, she would never quite finish the room. Chores like cleaning her room never seemed to get finished. She had to be continually reminded to finish the task at hand. The professionals called it attention deficit disorder, or ADD.

On the other hand, she loved to sit for hours and do crafts or puzzles. I deduced that if she liked doing something, she could spend hours on it, but if she didn't like it, she lost interest quickly—not unlike many adults I know!

Since it was hard for her to go outside, we encouraged her to do puzzles at the table. In no time she could do one hundred pieces. She went on to five hundred pieces, no problem, and today can do one thousand piece puzzles. We bought her a craft kit one year that had tiny pins and sequins in it. You had to put the pin in the centre of the sequin and pin it to a board to make a picture. Heather adored dolphins, so the first picture was a dolphin. She loved it, and sat for hours until she finished the picture. She also liked the Perler beads that you arranged on a plastic frame and then ironed to make a design. We put magnets on the back of her designs so she could display them on the fridge.

We always tried to get her to do her chores with the promise of a craft or puzzle afterward. Heather uses both hands equally well, but her left hand became dominant as she grew older. She tends to be a slow learner, but once she has it, she's got it for life. She doesn't forget anything.

She progressed to arm crutches around nine years of age. The idea was to wean her off all equipment. By the time she was in her late teens, she walked without any aid. However, she has now gone back to one leg brace and a rollator walker for stability.

We took Heather to London to ski when she was around twelve years old. She loved it. She used a sit ski where she sat in a bucket with skis on the bottom. It had a long rope out the back that her volunteer would hold on to. He could steer her left or right or slow her down.

It worked wonderfully and gave Heather a sense of motion. She also felt like one of the gang since her sister Leanne skied. She particularly enjoyed the hot chocolate time afterward, including lots of interaction with other kids.

Piano lessons helped Heather with her fine motor skills. She liked playing, but it was very hard for her to open her left hand, so we quit after a year.

Heather joined the disabled swim team at the Rotary Children's Place. There were no expectations of perfection—it was only to have fun and be part of a group. She also went there for the buddy swimming program. Aquatic therapy improved her muscle tone in her arms and legs. She would travel to different cities to compete with the team, and she earned medals and had a team jacket with "Iron Eagles" written across the back. The team met at a local gym on Tuesdays to work out with weights and cardio equipment. This group gave her a sense of belonging and self esteem. They played group sports as well. Heather entered several competitions and earned medals that she is very proud of. She loved being with the team and was very excited to get a medal.

Heather would also go to dances once a month at Grace United Church to meet other people and have a good time. Everyone was accepted; no one was turned away or left in a corner.

Being a teenager with spina bifida is very difficult. I'm sure there were times when kids were mean to Heather, and that hurt her feelings. She was very sensitive when kids weren't being nice, and she often had no sense of what the other kids were thinking about her. One of the reasons I wanted her to be like other kids was so they wouldn't make fun of her.

Heather went on to St. Pat's High School, where her program was again modified. She had a teaching assistant full time, and was matched up with a buddy who was in the regular school program. The "people program" really helped Heather become one of the gang. She ate lunch with all the children and wasn't segregated into a special section of the cafeteria. She was expected to go to her locker between classes to pick up the textbooks she needed for the next class. There were always teachers and aides on hand to help her if she got lost in the halls or didn't know what she needed for a particular subject. She stayed in high school for seven years so she could learn everything possible. This extra help prepared her for the next step, which would be Lambton College.

When Heather was around eighteen, the psychologist retested her. She told me that Heather would probably always function at the level of an eight to twelve-year-old. In spite of that, she graduated from St. Pat's High School with honours—a huge milestone that we celebrated with great pride and joy.

Yes, math is still hard for Heather, but she can balance her chequebook, and that's important. Heather lived at home while she attended college, so I had a nurse come in the morning to get her ready for school. We had made a separate apartment for her downstairs, where she had her own bedroom and washroom with a living room. The bus would come for her around eight in the morning and take her to the college. She took the early childhood education program. There was a special program called C.I.C.E. (Community Integration through Co-operative Education) where she was integrated into the normal classroom with an aide, who would take notes for her and help her with homework.

Heather loved the program because she was working with children and babies—something she loves to do. One of her assignments was to make age-appropriate toys for the children. That was a lot of fun for her. She painted wooden blocks as one of her projects. It's ironic that this was the same day care that Heather had attended when she was two years old, and now she was working for them and learning how to take care of babies and toddlers. Heather didn't graduate from this program because she missed too many days of school in her second year. She didn't complete a lot of the assignments that were required to graduate. However, she made a lot of friends with whom she still keeps in touch.

HEATHER GETS HER OWN APARTMENT

"I won't live forever," I told myself one day, thinking of what would become of Heather when I died. Heather needed to become independent from us, so I signed her up for assisted living in her own apartment. I wanted to be able to teach her how to live on her own while I was still alive.

When she was twenty-one, she moved into her own apartment, run by the March of Dimes, an organization that helps disabled people in the community who are eighteen years and older. Personal support workers went into her apartment daily to bathe Heather and prepare her meals. The first few years were difficult because she wanted to live with us. At first, we brought her home on weekends, and in the summer she got to come home for several weeks at a time. The problem arose when we tried to take her back to the apartment. She would kick and cry and refuse to get out of the car. We almost had to drag her to her apartment kicking and screaming.

I felt so awful. My heart was being pulled right out of my chest. I feared maybe the staff were abusing her. Was I doing the right thing? I knew other parents who still had their thirty-year-old disabled children living with them; however, they were having trouble coping with the physical and mental challenges of their children since their own health was also deteriorating due to age. We had to continually assure Heather that in a few days she could come back home. It took about three years before Heather stopped yelling and screaming when we took her to her apartment. This was a difficult time for us.

Now Heather is settled and likes her independence. She calls home every day, and knows we are only ten minutes away by car. Heather takes the disabled bus wherever she wants to go: shopping, doctor's appointments, bowling, outings with friends, and so on. She leads an active social life.

The internet has been very helpful in connecting Heather with her friends through Facebook, Messenger, and email. She can also look up recipes and print them off if she wants to do some baking.

Last Christmas, she learned how to knit scarves and hats on a round loom, and made matching hats and scarves for everyone as presents. Scrapbooking is another of her interests, and she once made a queen-size quilt. It took her three years, but she embroidered all the squares on her sewing machine and sewed all the blocks herself until she finally had enough pieces. We sewed little charms on certain squares as well. Another hobby she enjoys is word searches. She has recently taken up rug hooking, and has made a few beautiful rugs as presents.

Heather is passive in nature and would never start a fight. She never had any behavioural problems and didn't throw tantrums. She just cried if something was too hard for her. To this day, she is very determined and stubborn—she perseveres until she accomplishes what she wants. Wayne was a great support. I couldn't have done it without his help. He often came home from work to find the house in chaos and me in tears. He would take over by playing with the kids or taking them to the mall so I could have a break or a rest.

Even though I know God allowed Heather to be born into our family, I always felt guilty because I was the one who brought her into this world. All I could do was try to push her to her full potential. We always treated her like the other children. She had to do chores too—I wanted her to be as normal as she could be and not turn into a spoiled brat. People don't like a negative, selfish, angry person who feels hard done by or entitled to a better life. So I was determined that Heather would have manners.

Thankfully, Heather enjoys people and has no trouble talking. With her beautiful smile, she makes friends easily.

A poem called "Welcome to Holland" by Emily Perl Kingsley sums up the experience of having a disabled child. Kingsley describes having a baby like planning a once-in-a-lifetime trip to Italy—making plans, buying guidebooks, learning some phrases in Italian, and imagining all the sights you will see. But then just as your airplane lands, you realize that somehow you've arrived in Holland. Eventually you realize that although this is not what you've dreamed about for so long, Holland is still a beautiful and interesting place with many things to offer. They may not be the things you'd hoped to see, but you can still learn to enjoy the place where you are. She closes by writing,

…the pain of that will never, ever go away because the loss of
that dream is a very significant loss.
But if you spend your life mourning the fact that you didn't
get to Italy, you may never be free to enjoy the very special, the
very lovely things about Holland.[1]

---

[1] Emily Perl Kingsley, "Welcome to Holland," in *Chicken Soup for the Soul: Children with Special Needs*, edited by Jack Canfield, Mark Victor Hansen, Heather McNamara & Karen Simmons (Cos Cob, CT: Backlist LLC, 2012), pp. 2–4.

Heather taught me patience. I learned that Heather can live on her own and cope with life. She can speak up and tell people what she needs and wants. Wayne and I go to Florida for two months in the winter, and Heather has to fend for herself. We are in touch by email. Last February while we were gone, the staff at the March of Dimes Building where Heather lives told her she couldn't wash her back because she only had large rubber gloves and she needed medium gloves. I couldn't believe it. Heather solved the problem by going out to the drug store and buying some medium-sized gloves with her own money. She also had enough sense to take the receipt down to the Community and Social Services office to get her money back. I applaud her for thinking this through and not crying in a corner like she would have done ten years ago.

It's now 9 p.m. Wayne and I are totally exhausted and beyond worried about Darryl. "Has he survived? Will he survive?" The doctor appears at the door. We are the only ones in the quiet surgical waiting room, so we rush over to meet him.

The head transplant surgeon is still in his surgical garb, complete with hat, as he strides towards us. He looks exhausted. "We are just closing him up. The next twenty-four hours are critical. We don't know whether he will make it. We are taking him to the transplant ICU on the tenth floor. You can see him in about an hour. A nurse will come and get you."

"Where should we wait?" I blurt out, tears streaming down my face.

"Go and get some coffee and something to eat. It's going to be a long night. Go to the tenth floor waiting room."

When we arrive there, I continue reminiscing about our years with young children. We had always wanted a large family. We now had a healthy child—Leanne—and a special needs child—Heather. Should we go ahead and have another child, not knowing if the next one would be healthy?

CHAPTER THIRTEEN

Krystle

Wayne and I didn't want Leanne to be totally responsible for Heather after we were gone. Leanne was five and a half and Heather was three, so the spacing would be perfect to have another child. Wayne and I discussed it and decided to go ahead and try for another.

I got pregnant within a few months. It was a very emotional time. "Are we doing the right thing?" I often asked myself. I had all the blood tests and amniocentesis to ensure that the third child would be healthy. Amnio, as it is often called, is a procedure where the doctor inserts a needle into the amniotic fluid and removes some of it. The fluid in tested for any abnormalities. I didn't think about what I would have done if the tests had come back positive for spina bifida or some other condition. Could you abort a child from God? In any case, I wanted to know beforehand if the child I was carrying would be healthy so I could be better prepared. I'd been in shock when Heather was born with a disability. It was a long three weeks before the test came back. It was negative for any of the known diseases at that time, and we were relieved.

Leanne was very excited she was going to be a big sister to the baby. She had enjoyed the notion of Heather being born, but when Heather was whisked away right after birth, she'd felt cheated. Heather came home sick and Leanne couldn't touch her for fear of contaminating the incision on her stomach and head, although she had envisioned helping to change diapers and feeding Heather as well as holding her. Like all children, she thought Heather would be a great playmate right off the bat. Sadly, none of that came true.

With the coming birth of Krystle, Leanne felt that things would be different this time. She was older and would be able to take more responsibility with the new baby. She asserted that "Mom will be occupied with Heather still and she will need me more than ever."

Heather was very inquisitive about a baby sister coming. She constantly felt my tummy to see if she could feel the baby moving. Heather loved baby dolls and cuddled them whenever she played. She loved to feed them bottles and change their diapers. I felt she would be a good helper when the baby was born. The first thing she wanted to do was hold Krystle.

Krystle was born on November 11, 1983, Remembrance Day, and from the start, life was difficult. I was thirty-one years old when she was born. When you have two children, each parent gets one to take care of. When there are three, there's always one left out. It was hard having a baby to take care of with all of Heather's special needs as well. Even though Heather was three years old, she was still in diapers and needed help to eat, and we still had to do daily therapy at home as well. She had to have so many hours in her standing brace, and I had exercises for her muscles to keep them supple. Leanne was always the child who was left to fend for herself. Since she was already five years old, she could do most things for herself, like getting a snack, going to the bathroom, and getting dressed.

At five and a half, Leanne went to kindergarten every morning, so we had to be organized to walk her to the corner to catch the bus. Since Heather didn't walk, I put her in the stroller and had a front baby carrier for Krystle. It was really cold and windy in the winter, and getting the buggy through snow was difficult. I was exhausted every night. The house always looked like a disaster. I was too tired to even carry on a conversation with Wayne, so our relationship began to suffer.

Krystle was healthy, except that her legs were a bit bowed. At night, she had to wear special shoes with a rod in between her feet for the first three months. I can still hear her screaming. However, her legs straightened out, so it was all worth it. I nursed Krystle for ten months, then put her on the bottle. I felt I needed more time to myself. Wayne could feed her, or she could hold the bottle herself. Krystle grew normally and began crawling and then walking at the appropriate ages, with Heather following her around the house. Krystle quickly surpassed Heather's development, but she and Leanne were good with Heather and always shared their toys.

Around this time, I had been going to a Bible study with a lot of my close friends at the Missionary Church in Bright's Grove (affiliated with the Missionary Alliance of Canada). It was like a Pentecostal church. I also did some in depth Bible studies. These studies really helped me understand the Bible and what God was all about. We decided to join the Missionary Church as a family. Most of our close friends were going there as well.

It was a fantastic experience. The pastor would teach us about the scriptures and relate them to everyday life. I took lots of notes—it was like being back at school. Everyone in the church helped each other. If you needed an electrician, someone would volunteer; a plumber— someone would stand up, and so on. When people were going through hard times, the women would arrange for meals to be brought to their house. A calendar was passed around during the church service, and women would fill in the dates they could bring a meal to the family in need. We had a prayer chain where we would pray for certain people every day. I really felt we were in the best place of our lives.

When Krystle was about two, she fell off the bed and broke a bone in her leg and was in a cast for six weeks. It happened at night, so I had to go alone to the hospital with her screaming. It was stressful. The doctors put on a walking cast so it was a little easier for me; at least I didn't have to try and carry her and Heather at the same time. Heather walked a little by then, but she still preferred to crawl.

When I was at the hospital, the staff asked me about my other children. They noticed how stressed out I was. A few days later a social worker showed up at my door. The doctors at the hospital thought I had hurt Krystle and had reported me to the Children's Aid. I couldn't believe that they thought I was an unfit mother. I felt terrible. The social worker came to the conclusion that I was a good mother and they didn't take my children. All I could think was, *What next?*

When Krystle was almost four, I decided to send her to the French immersion school because I had always wanted to speak French fluently. I had spent a year in France and two months in Quebec trying to learn French, but I wasn't perfectly fluent. I figured it would be easier for Krystle since she would be starting to learn the language at an early age. I wanted my children to be bilingual so they could get a better job.

I had to have a meeting with the French school superintendent in order to get Krystle registered, as it was a Catholic school and we were Protestant. My taxes had to be switched to the Catholic Board. My mother was Catholic, so Krystle was granted acceptance. She had to take the bus to St. Thomas d'Aquin, but it was good because they picked her up in front of the house. She was a clingy child, and the first day the bus came for her she cried and screamed at her window seat as the bus driver shut the door. It was heart-wrenching to stand by helplessly, watching the bus drive off, and I bawled my eyes out. It took a few weeks before Krystle liked going to school.

Krystle liked playing soccer, and signed up when she was five years old. Leanne played at the same time. I stayed home with Heather while Wayne took them to their games.

The following year, Krystle's friend's dog had puppies. The kids desperately wanted one. "Can we go and just look at them, Mom?" they all chimed.

"Yes," I said reluctantly, "but we are only going to look." Famous last words; we came home with a little ball of fur. Jay was a six-week-old border collie and cute as a button. Krystle loved to take him on her paper route with her. When Jay was a little older and Krystle got rollerblades, she would strap on her blades and take him with her on the leash. It was fun until one day she came home with bloody knees.

My eyes widened when I saw her. "Whatever happened to you?"

She replied, "Well, we were on the side of the road, almost done the route, and Jay spied a squirrel on the grass heading for the nearest tree. He bolted, and since rollerblades don't do well on grass, I stopped dead in my tracks. I let go of the leash and he chased the squirrel right up the tree. Good thing we were almost home."

Krystle developed asthma in the winter months, but outgrew it until she was a teenager, when it returned even worse. She loved animals, and over the years we had a dog, rabbits, gerbils, and hamsters. Jay used to herd the baby bunnies in the backyard when we had them out of their cage. The animals were the worst thing for her asthma, but it was hard to say no to her. One time when we were cleaning out the electronic furnace filter we found a skeleton of a hamster that had gone missing one night. Mystery solved. Krystle had decided at a young age that she wanted to be a veterinarian, so all these animals were the perfect training for her.

Krystle did very well at school and she is now bilingual. She decided she wanted to go to an English-speaking school when she was going into grade seven, so she transferred to St. Anne's. She did very well there and graduated from grade eight with honours.

When she went to high school, she played on the school soccer team as well as the school hockey team. She made a lot of friends and enjoyed high school. The pet rat in the school lab had to come home from school for Christmas break. No one else would take it, so Krystle volunteered. We decided she would keep the rat in her bedroom so she could make sure it didn't escape. However, within a few days she became so allergic to it that she couldn't breathe. We had to take her to the emergency department where she was put on a drug to open her airways so she could breathe easier. The rat went to the Humane Society that very night. The school would have to replace it—Krystle's health was too important for us to keep it in the house.

The doctor kept Krystle in the hospital for a few days. She was scheduled to go back to school the next day to write an exam, but we had to reschedule it. She has an inhaler now when she plays hockey or runs.

Our pediatrician saw us weekly. He became a friend I could talk to about the problems I was having at home with the children. He would take time to listen to me, and he always said, "Keep up the good work, Mrs. Wallis."

Krystle graduated from high school and went on to the University of Guelph to study animal science. She did very well. However, veterinary school was difficult to get into. They didn't take many students. Krystle decided she didn't want to spend seven years at university; instead she got a job after completing her Bachelor of Animal Science. She has been working for a large feed mill company since graduating and has had several promotions. She is now working in the flour division with the same company. We are very proud of her.

Even though Krystle hasn't had to face the challenges Heather has in life, Krystle has challenges of her own, like asthma, that she has to overcome in order to live her life to the fullest.

"Mr. and Mrs. Wallis?" a nurse calls out.

We stand up and reply in unison, "We're over here."

"I'll take you to your son now." We quickly follow her down the hall to Darryl's room. There he lies with at least twelve intravenous lines coming out of his chest and arms. Numerous pumps control the dose of many drugs. He is so puffy I hardly recognize him. He has a breathing tube, so he can't talk, and he is also heavily sedated. We sit near the end of his bed and pray he will survive.

My thoughts drift to the upcoming summer, when we usually take the children to Algonquin Park camping. Will Darryl be able to go with us?

Chapter Fourteen

Camping Adventures

With three children, camping trips got a little more exciting. We had a pop-up camper now, and one summer we took it to Algonquin Park for two weeks. Leanne and Heather slept in one bunk, and Wayne and I slept in the other. It was Krystle's turn to be in the playpen.

One night, Heather suddenly yelled, "Dad, Dad, help!" Somehow one of the elastics that held the canvas down under her bunk had come undone. Heather had gotten wedged between the canvas and the bed and was hanging on for dear life to the edge of the mattress with her feet dangling outside the camper. She was rescued quickly before the bears could get her. She has never forgotten that night.

There are a lot of chipmunks in Algonquin Park. They even come up and eat right out of your hand. One day, we met a man who told us he'd had a favourite chipmunk that would come up to him and go into his pocket to get peanuts. One day he didn't realize that his little friend was behind him, and when he stepped back, he killed him. It was so sad to hear that story.

We took the kids to Algonquin Park every summer for two weeks. We liked Kearny Lake because the site we chose was right on the beach. We just had to go down a little trail and then we could sit on the beach and play in the sand and water. The children loved it. We were also close to the small creek that flowed into the lake. Krystle and Leanne would often go there to catch tadpoles and frogs in their nets, and at night they caught fireflies in jars. We always had a campfire each night where they roasted marshmallows and hot dogs before going to bed. If it was cold, we had hot chocolate with marshmallows. We really bonded as a family during these trips.

The number of stars up north was amazing. We could see all the constellations vividly, even the Milky Way. The children didn't like the long eight-hour car ride to get there, but when we reached our campsite, they were delighted.

Right after supper we would go to the outdoor theatre. We sat on benches to watch a slide show on some aspect of the park. A particularly interesting one was on bears in Algonquin—the ranger had slides of real live bears making a den to hibernate for the winter. In February they had their cubs. They emerged from the den in April or May to forage for food after the long winter.

There was usually a movie too, after the slide presentation. One night it was about Tom Thomson, the painter from the Group of Seven, who spent a lot of time painting the landscape of Algonquin Park. Heather or Krystle would usually be asleep by the time the program was over and we would have to carry them to the car.

One time we saw a mother bear on one side of the highway with a cub; the other cub was across the road. All the cars on Highway 60 were slowing down to see what was happening. The mother bear became increasingly frantic as more people showed up. She was making this loud bawling noise, trying to get her cub to follow her. Finally, the lone cub crossed the highway to the mother and they all took off into the woods.

There is a logging exhibit in Algonquin Park where children can climb all over the machines and watch a short movie. There are buildings to visit that represent the time when the park was used strictly for logging. Another interesting thing to do is visit the museum where real animals found dead in the park are displayed in dioramas. The museum is an interactive area for visitors to see how Algonquin is today, as well as what it was like hundreds of years ago. Every year we would visit both exhibits, and the children looked forward to these outings.

There are over ten hiking trails in Algonquin Park, varying in length from one kilometre to ten. Each year we would go on a lot of the hikes and guided walks that the park offered with knowledgeable naturalists. The children really enjoyed the insect walk where they could hold all sorts of bugs. Once a week, the rangers took us on a canoe outing down the river. We loved those excursions because we usually saw otters, hummingbirds, and kingfishers. We learned about aquatic plants like waterlilies and sundew. The sundew plant catches flies and insects to eat on its sticky surfaces. The children also loved to ride their bikes around the campground searching for treasures. It was a safe environment.

Once when Heather was seven years old, we decided to go to another campground in Algonquin Park called Achray, in order to go on a hike with Leanne, Heather, and Krystle. Heather's McLaren buggy would not go on this trail, and she was too heavy to carry. We told her she would have to walk holding her dad's hand for support. She agreed and off we went. Leanne and Krystle ran ahead of us, and I tried to keep up with them while Wayne lagged behind with Heather.

Sometimes when we camped close to home at Ipperwash or Pinery Provincial Park, Grandpa and Grandma would come up for the day and enjoy a campfire and meal with us. There was a store nearby where we walked to get ice cream.

Even as the children have grown and gone out on their own, those camping trips provided us with so many adventures that have become precious memories we will hold dear all of our lives.

CHAPTER FIFTEEN

Memories of Grandpa and Grandma

Wayne's dad, the kids' Grandpa Jiggs, loved ice cream and he often made milkshakes after supper. He always added a banana to make it thick and delicious. Sometimes at night Grandma would make us hot chocolate. The kids loved to go to the farm, where they could run around freely and pet all the kittens. There was always a dog there, too. As I explained earlier, Heather was afraid of the animals, but the other kids liked them. Heather was on the floor most of the time and the big golden retriever would come over and lick her face. She was scared he was going to eat her.

Wayne's mom and dad moved off the farm in 2001, a year before Jiggs died. The new house was smaller, so they held a big auction of all their possessions at the arena. They sat in the front row so they could see how much money they would get for each item. I bought most of the things like the bedroom sets and rocking chairs because I believed those antiques should stay in the family. I even have the Victrola that belonged to Jiggs' dad. It was full of records in their original cases, and

Wayne's grandpa had handwritten the album names on the outside of the envelopes they were stored in. This was very special to me.

Grandpa's heart got weaker as he aged. One day, at age eighty-seven, he told his wife that his stomach didn't feel good. He had been up most of the night in pain. An ambulance was called and he was transported to the London Hospital. Mary thought she would go to the hospital later in the afternoon since she had not gotten much sleep the night before. While he was in the ambulance he suffered a fatal heart attack. He was pronounced dead when he arrived at the hospital with no family at his side. We still miss him dearly.

Living in the city was a change for Mary. She got to know her close neighbours quickly. Her garden was smaller—pretty much just big enough to grow some tomatoes. A neighbour boy cut her grass, which was quite different than someone in the family having to ride the lawn mower around their big property. Despite the changes, she enjoyed the new house.

Mary met a man named Ron whom she had known when she was younger. He had lost his wife and was looking for companionship. They enjoyed going to play euchre together on Thursdays each week. They kept each other company for a few years until Ron was diagnosed with cancer and died a few months later. Mary was very sad. She had been in the house for six years at that point.

At Christmas, her memory started to fail her. A few months later in 2009, she was diagnosed with a blood disorder, acute amyloid leukemia. There was no cure, and at the age of eighty-seven, the same age her husband Jiggs had been when he passed away, she died peacefully in the hospital surrounded by her family.

Darryl survives the first night after surgery, with Wayne and me sleeping at the foot of his bed. It's barely 6:30 when the transplant surgeon strides into our room the next morning. "If he makes it through the next forty-eight hours, he has a good chance," he says with guarded optimism.

Chapter Sixteen

Darryl

We'd always wanted four children. I had read a lot of books about raising children and didn't want Heather to be the middle child—they usually have the most problems growing up because of their position in the family. So Wayne and I decided to have another child. I didn't have amniocentesis for this pregnancy but I did have blood tests to determine if the baby had spina bifida. All the tests were normal.

Darryl was born a little sooner than planned. His due date was February fourteenth, and he came on January twenty-fifth, 1986. Darryl's middle name, William, was chosen in honour of my dad, who had died before we got married. Krystle and Darryl were just two years apart, so we now had four children under seven. Yikes, what was I thinking?

Everyone was elated to have a baby boy—there hadn't been a boy born in Wayne's family for at least thirty years. Wayne's parents were the first to arrive at the hospital a few hours after Darryl was born. I had nursed all the kids, and Darryl was no exception. The only problem was that he wanted to eat every two hours. I started him on Pablum a little sooner than the girls; after all, he was a boy and maybe he would eat more.

I trusted our pediatrician to guide me with Darryl's care. I spent many days in his office. His secretary was very patient with me—I would call her about every little thing that I wasn't sure about, and she would always assure me that I was doing a fine job. It was comforting.

The acne on Darryl's face hadn't healed at six weeks, unlike most babies. He had scaly patches on his head, and the creases of his arms and legs had dry spots on them like eczema.

At three months old, Darryl's stools smelled very bad, and weren't forming in a pasty mush—they were liquid. I waited, and by four months his stools were frothy and awful-smelling. In fact, I had to take his diapers immediately to the basement and wash them out in the sink.

When Darryl was about five months old, I developed a constant sinking feeling. I knew something was wrong. When I was nursing Darryl, he would projectile vomit a lot. This was unusual, because breastfed babies usually tolerated their mother's milk well and didn't even spit up. His tummy was very large and distended—not soft like my other children's had been. My husband just felt I was nursing him too much and his stomach couldn't hold all the milk.

Our pediatrician did lots of tests. This started us on a roller coaster as one diagnosis after another was ruled out. He wasn't totally sure, but he thought Darryl had celiac disease. I looked up all the literature on celiac disease and was happy to find out that if I changed his diet, he would be fine. His pediatrician sent us to London, Ontario, which was about an hour's drive from our house. We had an appointment with an adult gastroenterologist to make sure our doctor's diagnosis was right. Darryl needed to have specially pre-digested milk that had to be ordered by the pharmacist. It cost a hundred dollars a can, and I wondered how we would pay for this.

Darryl smiled and babbled at the appropriate age. He played with his food a lot instead of eating it. He didn't sit at six months like most of my friends' children, although he walked when he was one.

His sisters had fun with him. They liked getting him dolled up in dresses and playing house. As a child, he liked to play with Lego. He loved books and began reading at age three. His favourite books were about Clifford the Big Red Dog.

He seemed to have a lot of ear infections, so eventually the doctor put tubes in his ears. He couldn't hear properly and his tongue was tied, so he had speech therapy for a few years at the Rotary Children's Place, where he also had occupational therapy. He loved it when they would roll him on the big ball or let him crawl through the cardboard tunnel.

The doctor in London did more tests. He thought that maybe our son had pancreatic insufficiency—when the food isn't digested properly because the pancreas is lacking enzymes. The doctor gave him capsule pills, but Darryl was less than a year old and couldn't swallow capsules, so we broke them up and put them in applesauce four times a day. The pills started to eat away the skin around his mouth, which became very red—and his stools did not improve.

Darryl was well enough to have a big party for his first birthday. I was in a four-bed ward when he was born, and I'd gotten to know the other women in our room who'd had babies the same day. I invited them all, and everyone was having a great time—until something happened that brought the party to a screeching halt.

Darryl was climbing the three stairs from the family room to the kitchen at the same time as my friend was going up the stairs. Darryl got caught up in her long skirt and fell right on the steel bar on the edge of the stair. A large cut between his eyes immediately spurted out blood! I panicked, and Darryl was screaming. Luckily, another mom who worked at the school knew exactly what to do. She immediately put ice on the wound and applied pressure, then drove us to the hospital where Darryl received many stitches.

I was a wreck. Everyone else cleaned up the house and went home while I was at the hospital. I was thankful that they were so considerate.

THE NEW HOUSE

Wayne and I thought we needed a bigger house, so we began looking for a two storey, four-bedroom home with lots of storage for the children's things. We would all be on the same floor instead of having Leanne and Heather in the downstairs bedroom off the family room. We found one in April 1987 and moved in. It had a big backyard that was already fenced in. We had a railing installed going into the house so Heather could enter on her own.

Leanne and Darryl had their own rooms while Heather and Krystle had bunk beds together, leaving the master for us. It was fantastic. Wayne had always wanted a swimming pool, so in the spring of 1992 we had one put in with stairs and bars for Heather's ease of entry. We even put in a ledge in the deep end near the diving board in case she got into trouble. It was a seat that she could crawl up into, with a bar to get out of the pool. She loved swimming, and we knew the pool would help strengthen her muscles.

After Darryl came along, Wayne had to take Heather to her swim meets in Windsor, as well as driving Leanne and Krystle to all their soccer games. In addition, he would often take Heather to her doctor's appointments in London and therapy sessions in Sarnia.

Darryl, age 4 with the shirt and coveralls I made for him

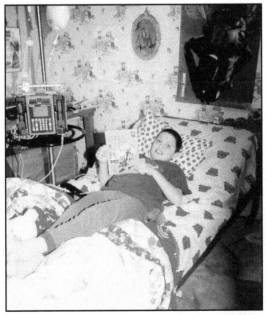

*Darryl, age nine, hooked up to the intravenous machine
every night in his room - 1995*

Krystle, Leanne and Darryl climbing the ramparts of a castle in Wales, July 2002

Visiting Judy, my best friend July 2005

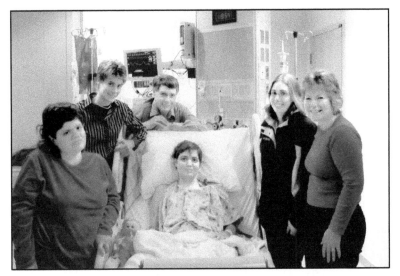

Christmas Day 2006, Darryl is one month post transplant

Darryl and Leanne, Christmas 2013

Heather with Christmas present, December 2014

Visiting Darryl, the pharmacist, at work, April 2015

Darryl runs through fire at the Warrior Dash, July 2017

Darryl's family: Jamie, Owen, Olivia, Darryl, October 2017

Owen on his third birthday with his Darth Vader cake, August 2019

*Annual Christmas photo, December 2019, Back row, Kevin, Kaleb, Heather,
Wayne, Leanne, Krystle, Front row, Darryl, Amber, Sandra, Owen, Alexi*

CHAPTER SEVENTEEN

Darryl's Health Deteriorates

Darryl stopped gaining weight shortly after his first birthday. The doctor in London told us to take him to Toronto. He said they had a pediatric gastro endocrinologist there who might be able to help, because he couldn't do anything more for him.

The adult gastroenterologist in London thought that a transplant of Darryl's bowel would help him to digest food, but no one was doing bowel transplants on children thirty years ago. They had just started doing some bowel transplants on adults at Toronto General Hospital, but most of the patients died.

When Darryl started eating food, he just vomited it all up. His doctor in London said if I could keep him alive for twenty years, then maybe he could have a transplant in Toronto. I knew then that keeping him alive and healthy was going to be the fight of our lives. However, I was up for the challenge and felt I could handle anything now after my experience taking care of Heather's needs.

I could never have imagined what was going to be our life for the next twenty years. Nothing could have prepared me for what I was about to go through.

By the time Darryl was around fourteen months old, he looked like a malnourished child with a big stomach, like the ones you see in the posters from Africa. Bones jutted out of his body. He didn't grow past eighteen pounds. I remember looking at him in the crib, able to see every vein in his body. His eyes were hollow—black circles surrounded the eye socket. They had no life in them. I couldn't believe my eyes. He couldn't even sit up or stand, he was so weak.

I had taken him to a chiropractor to see if he could work on the nerves in Darryl's back. He always went to the bathroom a lot when he came home from his appointment, but I could see no amount of therapy was going to cure him. I was really afraid he was going to die. I was at a dead end, and I often cried myself to sleep just worrying that he might not make it until morning.

We were scheduled for an appointment in Toronto at Sick Children's Hospital. The first doctor who looked at Darryl in the emergency department said that our son was wasted. Growing up in the sixties, I thought he meant Darryl was on drugs, so I assured him our son was not on drugs.

The doctor held up a hand. "Oh no, I mean he has no muscle tone."

Under other circumstances, the misunderstanding might have been funny.

Darryl was admitted to the hospital. After countless tests, the doctor said, "We think we know what he has, but we can't fix him."

I started to cry uncontrollably. I was devastated—deflated like a balloon.

So now we had a diagnosis. It was a rare disease. The doctors called it gastrointestinal pseudo-obstruction or hollow visceral myopathy. There were only two other cases in the world—I think a man in Australia and a young girl near Barrie, Ontario. Nothing was written up in the books, and there was no formal game plan, so to speak.

The girl from Barrie was a few years older than Darryl. She had similar problems, but they weren't identical. She died at the age of nineteen from complications with her heart (upon which I was devastated to think that Darryl could face heart problems in the future). Everything was trial and error with Darryl's medications and treatment. The goal was to keep him alive until a cure was found or a transplant could take place.

While Darryl was in the hospital, a lot of interns and residents did all sorts of tests on him to see if they could figure out anything else about his diagnosis. Nothing was ever discovered, and I wonder now why I put him through all that pain. At the time, I was clinging to hope that they would discover something new.

DARRYL NEEDS LIFE SUPPORT

I had been learning a lot of big words, given the mind-boggling number of specialists we'd had to see. Though I was a bit broken in because of Heather, I still had a lot to learn. I realized God was really in charge. The doctors, though some of them acted as if they were God, were really only caring human souls who tried their hardest to help us.

At eighteen months of age, Darryl fell out of bed and broke his collarbone. His arm was in a sling for several weeks. The doctor said it was normal, but after doing a bone scan they found that his bone density wasn't consistent with his age.

In August 1987, we faced an even greater trauma. My memory of those days is vivid. Here's how I recall it:

Darryl is now eighteen months old, and has stopped growing. He is rushed to Sick Kids in Toronto, and put on a specially-made intravenous mixture that gives him all the nutrients he will need to survive. It's called Total Parenteral Nutrition, commonly known as TPN. The nurses put an intravenous line in his arm, and over twenty-four hours they slowly give him the TPN. However, after only a few days, the intravenous solution leaks out through the veins and into his tissue. The nurses try several spots in both arms, but nothing seems to work for very long before Darryl's arm gets puffy with fluid. The doctors decide Darryl needs a permanent feeding line.

The prospect of a normal life for him has disappeared. Even if he has a successful transplant, a life lived on immunosuppressants will leave him with another host of issues, including greater risk of getting cancer. I am clinging to God's promise, *"I will never leave you nor forsake you"* (Joshua 1:5, NIV). The surgery to insert the line is tomorrow. Neither one of us gets much sleep this night.

Wayne and I hold Darryl's hand as he is wheeled into the operating room crying. He looks so small and angelic. We pray he will survive this operation to put a central venous line into his neck (little do we know that this is a routine surgery compared to what he will face in the future). The line pops out through his chest, and is stuck down with a sterile dressing and some special tape. The dressing needs to be changed every three days. A connection on the end of the line is hooked up to intravenous tubing and then into his TPN bag, which we hang on a pole. There is an intravenous pump that we set to infuse this food over several hours.

Darryl couldn't swallow pills. To strengthen his bones, the doctors gave him extra calcium in his intravenous food. Unfortunately, that caused kidney stones that were very painful. He had to go to Toronto for lithotripsy—a procedure to break up the stones into gravel that would sit at the bottom of the kidneys and not cause a problem.

It was decided that the only way Darryl could live was to put him on intravenous feeding twenty-four hours a day. No one had survived very long on intravenous feeding because it destroyed the liver. It was also very expensive. Fortunately, O.H.I.P., our provincial hospital plan, covered the cost of the medical supplies, but we still had to pay for the monthly trips to Toronto to the hospital. Miraculously, after three weeks he looked like a different child, so I never regretted taking him on the four-hour trips to Toronto. He had gained weight and was very happy. He played all the time instead of lying listless in his crib. Since Darryl liked to play with Lego, when he stayed in the hospital, the recreational therapist, Sarah, would bring him Lego sets, which he really enjoyed.

Darryl tried to eat food. He loved spicy food—he would put it in his mouth and chew it up, then spit it out. At that point, the intravenous food was taking care of his nutritional needs, and any food he ate was just to experience the different tastes and textures. We were so happy, and again thanked God for this miracle.

I had to be taught how to take care of the central venous line in Darryl's chest. At Sick Children's Hospital in Toronto, two excellent nurses spent a few hours with me every day for three weeks. The sterile procedure for changing dressings was the hardest for me to learn. Vitamins and drugs had to be mixed and administered. Supplies had to be ordered on time. I knew nothing about any of this.

While I was away at "class," Darryl spent time in the playroom with a volunteer named Dorothy. She was older, with grown children of her own. She had a soft voice and a kind face, and wore a yellow hospital gown. She rocked Darryl in the rocking chair and played with him on the floor, and he loved her. She was a godsend—the grandmother I needed for him, since my mom never came to the hospital. My mom said she didn't like hospitals. Well, who does?

One day, Dorothy invited me to her apartment to have lunch. I couldn't believe a stranger could be so giving. I really missed her after she left the hospital. She has now moved to Australia, but we keep in touch.

DARRYL COMES HOME

A nurse from Toronto was sent to our house before Darryl arrived home from the hospital. She set up all the necessary medical supplies in a dresser so it was easy for me to access them. She gave me her phone number so I felt at ease knowing I could call her at any time. Darryl was discharged once the nurses and doctors were confident I could take care of him.

I was really scared to take him home in case I made a mistake with these complicated procedures. However, his nurses assured me I could do it, and said I could call them any time. I did make some mistakes, like when Wayne and I both added his vitamins without realizing the other one had done it as well. Fortunately, there was no adverse reaction.

After six weeks, Darryl was gaining weight steadily, and was thriving on this new feeding method. There weren't very many children on intravenous at home thirty years ago, especially so far from Toronto. A few times, I was asked to speak to other parents about what it was like to carry out all these procedures at home. I assured them that they could do what had to be done, just as I had done at our house.

When we brought Darryl home after he got his central venous line, we decided to have a big party to celebrate. Everyone was invited—we must have had a hundred and fifty people at our house. All our friends, neighbours, and people from the Missionary church came bearing presents and food. The house was decorated for the celebration. I took lots of pictures and made Darryl a special album for his birthday present. Children were running everywhere. We were so happy and blessed once again.

A few times, Darryl's central venous line got blocked by a blood clot. This was dangerous and frightening because the clot could dislodge into his bloodstream and cause a stroke. I'd been sent home with special medication in case this happened—I had to mix it and administer it slowly into the line so it would dissolve the clot. It worked most of the time, but other times we had to go to Toronto and get a new intravenous line put in surgically.

One time, Darryl was in so much pain that the doctor sent me home with morphine. Darryl didn't like taking it because he said it made him feel weird. I didn't realize too much of the drug could kill him. I was taught how to crack the vial top off, draw up a certain amount of morphine, and slowly push it into his central venous line over so many minutes. A few days later, the doctor told me not to give him any more because someone had died at home due to too much morphine. That scared me.

Normally, I had to run two separate lines that were joined together with another connecting tube. He had one for TPN and then another one for the bottle of lipids, which were special fats. When he got sick, I had to join a third line for the drug. Calea Pharmacy would send another pump from Toronto to run the drug. I had to call the TPN nurse in Toronto, and she would walk me through how to set up the lines. I would have to draw pictures so I wouldn't forget.

Sometimes Darryl would get admitted to our local hospital by our pediatrician. Our doctor had taken a trip to the Toronto hospital to meet with Darryl's gastroenterologist to understand his condition and how to take care of Darryl's specialized needs. In Sarnia, there had never been a case like Darryl's. The nurses were afraid to take care of him, and I had to go over and instruct them on how to change his dressings and run his TPN. Everyone was gowned and masked, and sweat would be rolling down their faces by the time we were done. A lot of times, I would just go over and hook him up and run the drugs myself.

TRAINING WITH "DARRYL" THE DOLL

We had a doll made to look like Darryl. The doll had a hole in its chest with a central venous line sticking out. I used it to teach the nurses how to hook him up and do his dressings. I also took it to the school to show the teachers what Darryl looked like under his shirt and how to clamp his line with the special clamp if it ever broke while he was at school.

EQUIPMENT, SUPPLIES, AND SCHEDULING

Every week, a truck would pull up and unload about fifteen big boxes that would have to be put away in Darryl's room. His intravenous food was so heavy they could only put five days' worth in each box. The driver usually carried those upstairs for me because of the weight. In his room was also the thirteen-cubic-foot fridge and a hospital bed that elevated his head so the acid from his stomach wouldn't eat away his esophagus.

A man at Wayne's work made a special stainless steel plate where we could prepare Darryl's sterile lines and drugs. A table was donated to us for him to lie on while I hooked him up to his machine, enabling me to function more easily. The intravenous pump they sent home with me was different than the one I had trained on in the hospital, so another nurse came from Toronto and showed me how to use it. I also read the manual that came with it a few times. Every few years, the pump was changed and we had to learn how to use it all over again.

When Darryl got a blood infection, we had to have a separate pump to run the drugs and the bags of saline to flush the line between the TPN and the drug. The two pumps were heavy, so we asked for a different pole that held them side by side with several rolling wheels on the bottom instead of having the pumps on top of each other. This pole was much easier for Darryl to push around. Luckily, there was a bathroom right beside his bedroom so he didn't have to go downstairs. When it was time for supper, we would carry the intravenous pumps—with his TPN running—down the thirteen stairs to the kitchen so he could be with us. He never ate anything, but I thought it was important that we were all together at supper.

I taught Wayne how to take care of Darryl's dressings and how to run all his intravenous fluids. That gave me a much-needed break. When Darryl got older and stronger, he could carry his pumps downstairs by himself. He also learned how to hook himself up and run all his medications and then disconnect himself in the morning. A medical case full of supplies had to be with Darryl wherever he went. The nurses at Sick Kids in Toronto taught me what to pack in this case. A special clamp was attached to his shirt in case the central line broke while we were out—this clamp would stop the blood from coming down the tube.

Having the case along came in very handy on several occasions. One time we were in the car on the way to Toronto for a checkup, and there was a traffic accident somewhere up ahead of us. Wayne was driving, thankfully. Darryl had been vomiting quite a lot and was becoming dehydrated. His eyes were black underneath and sunken in. I was getting worried. Luckily, I had the red case with all the supplies I needed to hook him up to his machine. I quickly flushed the line with saline, hung the 500-millilitre bag of saline on the coat hook on the door, and hooked him up. A trip that normally took three and a half hours took six that day. When we arrived at the hospital, they decided to keep him for a few days to see what was going on.

It turned out that he needed his gallbladder out because it was full of gallstones. They operated laparoscopically and pulled the gallbladder out through tiny incisions in Darryl's abdomen. Two hours later, he was up playing pool in Marnie's lounge.

Chapter Eighteen

Learning to Cope
with Darryl's Health Challenges

The doctors suggested we move to Toronto to be close to the hospital. Remember, Wayne is from a town of 350 people, and he hates Toronto. His job was in Wyoming, ON. So we decided it would be better for us to stay in our home and make the monthly commute to the set of specialists Darryl now had in Toronto.

The urologist also suggested we catheterize him since his bladder was atonic and he would develop urinary tract infections if we didn't. (An atonic bladder has no elasticity—the bladder gets really full of urine, but Darryl would never feel the urge to urinate because his bladder muscles couldn't contract and signal that it was time for emptying.) We had to use a long plastic or rubber catheter tube and insert it into his urethra, and the urine would be drained into a dish. Most two-year-olds could hold about 150 ml of urine; Darryl could hold at least 800 ml. This procedure was done every four hours.

Unfortunately, Darryl seemed to get more infections when we started to catheterize him, so I decided to stop. The doctor wasn't happy with me and said if I didn't do what he recommended, then I couldn't take Darryl to him anymore. So we found a new pediatric urologist who would work with me and listen to my concerns and discuss things with me. Darryl learned to push out the urine rather than us having to catheterize him.

Not only did we have to feed Darryl every day, but we also had to be careful that he didn't get a blood infection or urinary tract infection. The pump would alarm many times in the night, and one of us had to get up and reset it. Sometimes his line would get kinked and the fluid couldn't get through; other times there was air in the line. A few times his line became totally disconnected from his body and blood would spill all over the floor. I sort of panicked when I first saw all the blood, but I knew I had to figure out what to do quickly or Darryl would bleed to death. I disconnected the broken line, flushed it with saline, and hooked him up with brand new lines.

Needless to say, we didn't get much sleep at night for many years. Even when Darryl got older and knew how to reset the pump at night when it alarmed, he was such a sound sleeper that he seldom heard the alarms

Wayne and I took turns resetting the pump and lines during the night. We would alternate hooking Darryl up nightly to his machines. I couldn't trust anyone else to care for him while I was in the house, although we did get funding for a nurse to come in and watch him while Wayne and I went out. It helped for the two of us to have some time to ourselves to work on our relationship.

Darryl also needed physiotherapy, speech therapy, and occupational therapy. Since he hadn't been developing normally before starting the intravenous, he was behind in his age group. Between Heather and Darryl's appointments, I was never home. Therapists say a special needs child is like having two children, so in that light, we really had six kids, not four.

INFECTIONS

One time, Darryl got a rare blood infection. He had to go directly to the hospital in Toronto. His blood was sent to the infectious disease lab in Ottawa to see if they could figure out what was causing such a high temperature. They discovered that it was a rare yeast growing in his blood. He was put on high doses of specialized antibiotics for three weeks in the hospital before they sent him home. I received homecare when I got home with Darryl. A lady would come in and make meals and clean the house. I appreciated her, and it was nice to have another adult to talk to.

Darryl needed to be on the expensive drugs for three more weeks when we got home, so homecare also sent a nurse to give him the drugs to kill this rare blood infection. Although I was quite capable, because the government was paying for the drugs (each dose cost more than $600), they wanted to make sure they were correctly administered. It was ridiculous, since the nurse had no idea how to mix or give the drugs and I ended up having to teach her.

A TRIP TO DISNEY WORLD

When he was six years old, Darryl was chosen by the Sunshine Foundation to go on a family trip to Disney World in Orlando, Florida. Someone suggested we send the intravenous food by FedEx so it would be there when we arrived instead of taking it on the plane. No one had ever done a Disney trip before while on intravenous feeding, and when the food arrived at the airport, no one knew what to do with it, even though it said *Keep Refrigerated* on the boxes. Some of the boxes had split and the food was oozing out the sides by the time we arrived, and the temperature was about a hundred degrees Fahrenheit. So again, more food had to be made in Toronto by Calea, our pharmacy in Mississauga, and sent to our hotel in Florida. They also shipped us extra bags of saline because we had to use up our supply to keep Darryl from getting dehydrated while we waited.

CAMPING

Sometimes Heather would go to the Easter Seal camp in London for two weeks while we took the other kids camping. Again, we hired a nurse from Sick Children's Hospital to come to the house so Darryl could stay home in a clean environment instead of a sandy campsite. Those times, we only took Leanne and Krystle. It was much easier, and it gave us more time to spend with the two kids who often got overlooked while we were tending to the needs of Heather and Darryl. Sometimes we took Heather too, and just had time with the girls, as well as opportunities to catch up on sleep without the pump alarm going off in the night.

However, we missed being all together on our camping trips. We felt Darryl was missing out on the outdoors. He liked the idea of camping, but didn't enjoy mosquitoes. We decided to go to Algonquin Park in August when there were fewer bugs. We packed our winter coats because it sometimes got down to eight degrees Celsius at night at that time of year.

Darryl really blossomed when we figured out how to take him to Algonquin Park in our pop-up camper. Before we left, we organized all his medical supplies for each day in Ziploc bags. In Algonquin Park, he was away from schoolwork, television, and video games. He was free to fish, collect acorns, chase chipmunks, go for walks, or just read a book. He usually slept in the car during the eight-hour trip to the park.

We bought an electric cooler that we could plug in for Darryl's intravenous food. Though Kearny Lake, our campground in Algonquin, didn't have electricity, there was power in the comfort station that had just been built. We asked the campground hosts if we could store his food in the utility shed while we were at the park, and they said yes.

The shed was locked, so we didn't need to worry about anything happening to the food. We had a key made so we could get his food when we needed to hook him up at night. This arrangement worked fine for a few years, until the park decided storing the food in the utility shed wasn't allowed anymore. They said we could take the cooler to the park office and plug it in there. Unfortunately, during one cold night, the ranger put the cooler too close to the baseboard heater and it melted the transformer. We had to go out and buy a new transformer, which cost about two hundred dollars. Luckily the park paid us back for it. All this work was worth it though, because we could be together as a family.

We always had campfires, and often stared up at the sky, admiring all the stars. It was so dark away from all the city lights that the stars really stood out and the Big Dipper was easily visible.

Darryl was hooked up to his machine around 6 p.m., so he watched from inside the camper as we told stories and roasted marshmallows around the bonfire. We felt sorry for him, so we devised a makeshift intra-venous pole from a tent pole. We secured it with a rope and a peg hammered into the ground. We could hook his pump onto it, and as long as he didn't move out of his chair, he was fine for a few hours outside. We made good use of cup hooks in the roof of the camper and in hotel rooms when we had to hang the bags of fluid that he needed to survive.

DISPOSITION HELPS WITH COPING

Darryl played well with other children and was very patient. He tried to help Heather with crafts that were too hard for her, and they'd spend hours together. He liked to do puzzles too, so they spent a lot of time together at the dining room table.

Darryl loved to read books, often reading with a flashlight while everyone else was asleep. He had a paper route when he was ten years old. When he was sick, Wayne or I had to deliver the papers. He hated doing the collecting, but enjoyed meeting his customers. We were trying to let him be like anyone else in the family.

Our son was a quiet child. He had good manners and was thoughtful and sensitive. If his siblings were fighting or crying in the house, he would start crying too. The conflict bothered him. To this day, you will never see him angry or fighting with anyone.

WHO KNEW AN ELECTRIC COOLER HAS A HOT AND COLD SETTING?

Wayne decided that, since the kids were getting older, he wanted to take a family camping trip out west to show the children the mountains in Alberta. In August 1994, Leanne was sixteen, Heather fourteen, Krystle eleven, and Darryl nine. We thought it might be our last family trip all together.

We ventured as far as Calgary, where something unexpected happened. We were staying in a hotel and the maid unplugged Darryl's food cooler by mistake. We had gone to Drumheller that day to see Dinosaur Provincial Park. When she plugged the cooler back in, she switched the hot side on instead of the cold side, and all his food was destroyed.

I couldn't believe it. How could this have happened? I hadn't even realized that the cooler could switch to being a heated box by reversing the plug. It was a nightmare. Calea Pharmacy was closed, so we called the next morning, hoping they could fly some more food to us in Calgary. They said they would have to send it by truck, and it would be three days before it arrived. In the meantime, we had to administer saline instead just to keep Darryl hydrated. Extra bags of saline were shipped with his food to replenish our supply.

Staying in Calgary an extra three days meant we didn't have time to go all the way out to British Columbia as we had planned. We thought a day trip up to Banff and Jasper to see the Columbia Icefields would be fun. When we arrived at the ice fields it was pouring rain so we couldn't go on them. What a disappointment!

When we picked up Darryl's food in Calgary at the depot, we decided to go to Waterton Lakes National Park as our last stop before we headed home. Oh, did I mention we were pulling our pop-up camper? Well, when we got to Waterton Lakes it was getting colder, even though it was the middle of August. In the morning when we awoke there was eight inches of snow on the ground. Talk about shocked! We had set our regular cooler outside the camper, and in the morning everything was frozen solid. The cows in the field had snow piled up on their backs. Everyone was happy to pack up and head home. We arrived home safely with no further mishaps a week later.

In 1998, a few of my closest friends saw an article in a magazine about a "Caregiver of the Year Award" given by Allianz Canada in Toronto. They immediately thought of our family, and each wrote letters explaining the selfless dedication and caring that Wayne and I were giving to our family. Out of all the submissions, our family was chosen to receive the award. It was quite an honour. We were given a certificate and one thousand dollars. One of the letters reads as follows:

I have known Sandy and Wayne for 24 years. Sandy's second child had Spina Bifida and Hydrocephalus. Countless hours of therapy, both in the home and at the Rotary Centre, were given to Heather. There were many monthly visits to London,

Toronto and Montreal for assessments. Although the doctors stated that Heather would never walk, Sandy never gave up her faith that Heather WOULD walk. Heather is 17 now and walks unaided.

Sandy's fourth child had major medical problems. This required regular trips to Toronto. Sandy and Wayne continued to pour out their love for Darryl and went above and beyond in their physical ability to care for him. Most parents would not have the energy to continue like they have. He was diagnosed with a rare disease called Gastrointestinal Pseudo Obstruction. A tube was placed in his neck and he was fed intravenously. Darryl grew, but continued to vomit daily. Every time he was sick, Sandy went with him to Toronto Sick Children's Hospital.

Wayne took care of the chores at home as well as working full time. He learned to give enemas to Heather and catheter her. When Heather went for operations, Wayne learned how to hook Darryl up and give intravenous drugs. The intravenous machine has problems nightly, which requires Sandy or Wayne to get up and fix it. Darryl also vomits during the night, which requires attention.

Sandra and Wayne have always tried to include their special needs children in a normal lifestyle. They take all four children camping with Darryl on life support.

There has been a tremendous amount of stress put on Sandra and Wayne in the past 20 years of marriage. They have persevered without complaining and only state that is what any parent would do for their children. They want all their children to reach their full potential and be a benefit to society.

Signed,
Debra A. Smith

LOSING HOPE

When Darryl was fourteen years old, he became so sick that he missed forty-six days of his first semester at school. Every time he got really sick, my heart became sad. This time, the doctors at the hospital in Toronto didn't even know what to do for him. His temperature was extremely high. They said his system was just shutting down and that this was the natural progression of his disease.

I prayed hard, and all our friends prayed too. Darryl asked me, "Am I going to die?" My heart sank to the lowest point ever. I said I didn't know.

The doctor arrived and I went out in the hall to talk to her. I said, "You can't let him die—there must be something you can do."

"There is nothing more we can do," she said.

This can't be happening, I said to myself. Where was God now? I was alone and afraid. Then, in the middle of the night, Darryl's fever broke and I was able to tell him he was not going to die that night. I thanked God for answering our prayers.

Our son spent a lot of time in his room. Thankfully, he liked mind games like Clue and Battleship, and Krystle or Leanne would take turns playing with him. He loved baseball and collected the cards, memorizing players' statistics, names, and which teams they played on. We got him a television for his room so he could watch baseball games, and he also liked to play video games.

He would always do his homework right after school when he got home. He was a good student, very courteous and well respected by his peers. All his teachers loved him. No matter what was going on inside his body, he always had a smile on his face. He excelled in science and math, and in high school he was part of the science fair that competed in Windsor (a city about one and a half hours from Sarnia) each year. When he was in Grade Eleven and Twelve, he was asked to tutor some students after school.

Darryl reviewed his school work every night. He always competed for the top marks in every class, and was on the debating team in high school. He got unhooked from his machines at 7 in the morning, and when he got home at 3 p.m., he was hooked back up. Sometimes we would carry his pumps downstairs to the family room so we could all watch a movie together.

Darryl had stopped eating regular food shortly after he went on intravenous feeding, but we still encouraged him to join us for meals. One day I asked him, "If you could have anything in the world, what would it be?"

He said, "I'd like to be able to eat real food." It seems we always want something we don't have, and Darryl was no exception.

ACTIVITIES

We wanted all the children to be brought up without restrictions as much as possible. Leanne got a paper route when she was ten years old, and when she went into high school it was passed on to Krystle. When Krystle was in high school, she passed it on to Darryl.

Darryl also wanted to be in the band at school. He was in grade seven at the new junior high school that the French Catholic Board had built. He chose to play the trumpet. Practice started at 7 a.m., so we had to run Darryl's food a little faster the night before and drive him to school instead of him taking the bus. He practiced at home every night. It was a proud moment to watch him play in the school concerts. He was all dressed up in a white shirt, tie, black pants, and dress shoes. After a couple of years of early mornings, he had to quit the band. He was disappointed, but it was just too much for him with everything else that was going on with his health.

Krystle and Darryl also took piano lessons during school hours. Watching them perform at the Sarnia Library was exciting. Sometimes when Darryl was at the hospital in Toronto, he was lucky enough to go to a hockey or baseball game with a few other sick children. Sponsors would donate a company suite to the kids for a night where they fed them pizza, pop, ice cream, and popcorn. Unfortunately, Darryl couldn't have any of it. I usually went with him, so I'd eat his share.

At Christmas, the Spina Bifida Association in London would invite us for a dinner at the Moose Lodge, complete with turkey, a decorated tree, crafts, and presents from Santa Claus. The meal was always delicious, and our children had a great time.

When I was young, I liked to sew and bake cookies. I wanted to teach my kids the same skills I had, so we would all make cookies together. Darryl was very precise in rolling the balls of gingerbread dough so all his cookies came out the same size. He never forgot how to make them from year to year. We also used to make hand-sewn Christmas ornaments. I remember one year all the kids made stuffed dinosaurs with red hats for the tree. They were really cute. Leanne made a small stuffed teddy bear. Krystle didn't like sewing very much, but did manage to make some beanbags for school one time that were filled with sand. She used my sewing machine while I was out shopping. She didn't realize that the sand dulled the blade on the serger—a special type of sewing machine—so I was a little angry with her when I got home.

Darryl did have limitations. He loved to play baseball, but wasn't allowed to slide into second base or home plate, which was almost a prerequisite to play. He was a great skier and learned fast; however, he wasn't allowed to do it for very long. His spleen was enlarged and it became very dangerous for him to play sports, because if he fell while skiing or was hit by a baseball directly to his spleen, he would likely bleed to death right there.

Wayne took him to his baseball games. They didn't tell me until recently why Darryl had to walk to first base one game. I thought it was because the pitcher threw four balls that were outside the strike zone. What really happened was that the pitcher hit Darryl! If I had known that, I wouldn't have let him go back.

Darryl was very private about his medical condition. He didn't want anyone else to know about all the tubes under his clothes that he needed to survive—he wanted to be treated like everyone else. He had a few close friends who knew about his medical issues, and sometimes they would come over after school to play video games with him while he was hooked up. I always made cookies for his friends, which they enjoyed.

NAVIGATING THE BUREAUCRACY

I found it difficult to get the funding for Darryl's special equipment, primarily his portable backpack, which carried his intravenous food and drugs as well as the intravenous tubing. I hated dealing with the bureaucracy. The first person I called was never able to help me; I was always transferred to several people or agencies before I got what I needed. It was so frustrating! I almost wrote a book on "how to manoeuvre your way through government agencies to get funding for your disabled child," except that I was too busy looking after my disabled children to write it. I spent hours on the phone every day.

Everyone had their mandate, and it seemed as though Darryl fell between the cracks. Sometimes he would have to go to Toronto weekly to see various specialists, and it was expensive for gas and accommodation as well as food. We were always short of money, which placed a big strain on our marriage. After I'd come back from grocery shopping, Wayne would ask, "Well, did you get everything?"

I would always reply, "I never get everything—there is only so much money." We always paid cash for groceries.

After all those trials and tribulations, though, Wayne and I are still together and we are happier than ever having survived these challenges. Quite a few of the parents I met at the Rotary Children's Place have gotten divorced. Usually the husband couldn't stand the stress of having an imperfect child, or didn't want to take on the extra work to take care of him or her.

CHAPTER NINETEEN

Keeping Darryl Alive and Teaching Heather Life Skills

I didn't know why God had given me two special needs children, but I was going to do everything in my power to make them independent and not a burden on society. How many people go through life thinking, *Why am I here? What is my purpose?* Mark Twain said the two biggest days in your life are the one when you are born, and the one when you figure out why. I believe one of my purposes in life was to keep Darryl alive until he could get a transplant.

It was also my purpose to teach Heather life skills so she could function on her own. I wanted her to have good social skills so that people would like her and help her if she needed it. A lot of people don't know what to say to a disabled person, so they just ignore them.

I wanted her to have money skills so she would be able to pay for things and not have people take advantage of her. She can count to twenty and recognize some bills, but cannot count very well. I got her a debit card when she moved into her apartment so she wouldn't have to carry cash around. However, a salesperson at the nearby mall once took advantage of her and sold her $1100 worth of specialty facial products.

Other so-called friends took her debit card and paid for pizza, beer, and cigarettes without her knowing.

Today she has a daily limit on her account and only gets a little bit of money each week so that the same thing doesn't happen again. However, recently a lady in her apartment building scammed Heather out of $1000 over a period of several months by telling her she needed food and diapers for her three children. She would take Heather in her wheelchair to the local ATMs and have her withdraw money. The woman also took her to the grocery store and had Heather pay for her groceries. She even took Heather's laundry money, food right from her refrigerator, and her bus pass, which forced Heather to cancel her doctor's appointments. I don't know how those people sleep at night.

Heather has a big heart, and when she sees someone in need, she doesn't understand that they are using her. She just wants to please them and have them as her friend.

The police suggested I take charge of all Heather's finances, buy her groceries, and take care of her medical bills. Heather has lost her independence due to others taking advantage of her. It's sad, but some people just don't have a conscience or compassion for those less fortunate. It has also put a lot of stress on my husband and me as we have to take care of all of her needs. Thankfully, she has just gotten a support worker who can take her grocery shopping.

I felt it was important for me to instil in Heather that she should ask for what she needed and not be afraid. When I was at our chiropractor one day, he said, "You don't have to worry about Heather. She can manage to get here on her own and tell me what she needs." The dentist had told me the same thing, and that made me feel good. I wanted my children to grow up to be strong and independent, and I have tried my best to accomplish this.

THE IMPORTANCE OF A CHURCH FAMILY

Our family had been going to the Missionary Church in Brights Grove, and we had all become Christians. Our church family helped us out tremendously with babysitting, prayers, meals, and more. I didn't have to worry if I needed to rush Darryl to the hospital in Toronto; I knew someone would bring a hot meal for the rest of my family. We couldn't have survived without their help. Looking back, I realize God was blessing our family through our church, reminding us that He was taking care of us.

Our pastor would often come to our house and pray with us. We learned over time that God sometimes says "no" to our requests and prayers. He sees the big picture of our lives. I believe God wants me to write this book to encourage other moms going through life and death situations with their children. He wants us to pray about everything we need, even if it seems impossible in our minds. We need to slow down and listen to God.

The Bible phrases that God always brought to my mind were, *"Be still, and know that I am God"* (Psalm 46:10, NIV), *"...with God all things are possible"* (Matthew 19:26, NIV), and *"I can do all things through Christ who strengthens me"* (Philippians 4:13, NKJV). I had the whole church praying daily that Darryl would survive. It reminded me of the verse that says *"...where two or three are gathered together in My name, I am there in the midst of them"* (Matthew 18:20, NKJV). I think this means that Jesus is always with us.

TRAVELLING BY AIR

Darryl's pediatrician would come to the house and check on Darryl when he was really sick. A few times, he had to order an air ambulance to take Darryl to Sick Children's Hospital in Toronto. That was always frightening. I had to pack the necessary supplies quickly for the trip, and I always took the red case which was filled with extra supplies.

One September, I remember taking a helicopter to Toronto. Darryl was about nine years old. The fall colours were beautiful and we were flying really low. I thought we were flying low so we could see the leaves on the trees, but they said no, due to Darryl's condition they couldn't fly very high. We landed at the island airport where an ambulance was waiting to take him to the hospital. A nurse accompanied us on that trip. I felt scared because I didn't know if he was going to survive.

Another time (about three years later) when Darryl had blood coming out of his stomach tube, we flew by airplane from Sarnia to

Toronto. It was pouring rain and I was a little worried about the storm. The plane was very small.

A nurse was with us that time too, so I felt a little better. The pilot radioed ahead to Toronto and told them when we would arrive. We took off with Darryl hooked up to an intravenous machine from the hospital. There was a lot of turbulence, and the pump alarm kept going off. Finally the nurse just shut it off. Darryl was dehydrated and he needed the fluids, but there wasn't anything she could do. I was in shock, because she didn't tell me what she was going to do about the blood that was now backing up in his line.

Luckily, I had his medical case and was able to fill his line with saline and put some heparin into the line so it wouldn't get blocked with blood. It was raining so hard that the radio stopped working as well. I began to wonder if we were going to make it. It was the trip from hell. I remember thinking, *What more could go wrong?* I shouldn't have asked, because at that moment the wiper blades quit working. All I could do was pray we would get to Toronto safely. We finally arrived—later than scheduled, but we were safe. An ambulance was waiting on the tarmac to drive us up to the hospital, and I thanked God.

MY FEELINGS

When Darryl was really sick, I felt dead inside. Everything was black, and I had trouble seeing past the next second. I lost hope. When he had to be admitted to the hospital in Toronto, I had nobody to support me, and even though there were people around me I felt so lonely and isolated. No one really understood what I was going through; let alone what Darryl was experiencing. My friends would say, "Everything will work out," but I didn't believe them.

From an early age, the doctors tried Darryl on several medications to see if they would help him digest his food, but nothing worked. Every time we saw a new doctor, he or she would make a different diagnosis. It was very frustrating because Darryl got sicker with every new medication.

Around seventeen months of age, Darryl was transported by ambulance to Toronto Western Hospital, where a specialist did some sophisticated tests and found that his nerves and muscles didn't work from the middle of his chest down. He had no peristalsis movement in his stomach or bowel. (Peristalsis is the wavelike contraction and relaxation of muscles to move food through your intestines.) In fact, all Darryl's organs were affected. His bladder would just fill up with urine and he never felt the urge to go to the bathroom. To prevent urinary infections, we would just tell him to go to the bathroom every few hours and try to push it out. His bowel movements were liquid. At night, he had to wear diapers. That was fine when he was under three years old, but it was embarrassing for him during his teen years.

I had hoped for a "normal" family, but that hope disappeared when we had two children with special needs who required a lot of time and energy. It broke my heart to see our only son not living the normal life that I had envisioned for him—no going out at night, no dates, no going for walks around the block.

As he got older—now fourteen years old—Darryl wanted to go out at night with his friends. I called Sick Kids Hospital and discussed the situation with them. They had one portable pump at the hospital that went inside a backpack. We could borrow it for a weekend. The tubing was expensive—twenty-five dollars a set—so it was important to hook up the lines properly without any mistakes that would destroy the lines. Eventually we bought our own portable pump. The Lion's Club of Wyoming, Ontario gave us money to buy some tubing one time, which was very generous.

At around age sixteen, Darryl learned how to do all his dressings lying down on his bed, run his intravenous food, and mix and run his drugs by himself. This lightened our load and gave Wayne and me a much-needed break. I was also glad because I felt it was important for Darryl to become independent. After all, he wanted to go to university, and would have to be able to take care of himself.

STRESSES OF OTHER CHILDREN

I knew I was neglecting the other kids, since Darryl's medical needs took a lot of time and energy. There just wasn't enough of either to go around. I would help them with their homework and piano practice as much as I could, and Heather needed to be taken to many therapies at the Rotary

Children's Place as well. It became especially overwhelming once we had three teenage girls.

I didn't realize Leanne was having a difficult time at school emotionally. She got great marks, but something was wrong. All teenagers seem to have a rough time growing up, and she was no exception. She had some counselling and definitely felt better after talking things over with the counsellor, which made me happy for her.

That's really the hardest part about having a child—or two—with special needs. It's not only they who are affected, or us, but the other children in the family too. All we could do was spend as much time with Leanne and Krystle as possible, then pray that God would help them and keep them safe and out of trouble.

LEANNE BLOSSOMS

Leanne was an honours student. We were so proud of the fact that she made the dean's list every year at high school. She wanted to be a lawyer. One summer Leanne thought she would try rugby. She found it much rougher than soccer, and always came home with tons of bruises on her legs.

When Leanne turned eighteen she went off to the University of Toronto to take criminology. She excelled in her studies. She always had a part-time job as well to help pay for things. One particular job she liked was being a chef at a bar because she could be creative with the food. After she graduated, she wrote the LSAT exam and passed with flying colours. However, she decided not to be a lawyer after all. The lifestyle of lawyers didn't appeal to her—she preferred to work outside.

Leanne got an office job for a while, but didn't like working inside, so she took a job near Hurst, Ontario to plant trees. One night when she was sleeping in her tent, a bear tore the end flaps right off of it. She was petrified that she could have been mauled to death. After that night she slept in the kitchen, which was the only wooden structure there. A few days after the scare with the bear, the guard dog at the camp bit her and broke the skin. When her contract was up in August, Leanne received a bonus and immediately took the first train home.

Picking apples in the Okanagan Valley appealed to her, so off she went to British Columbia in September. She thought this area was the most beautiful place on earth. She liked to travel, though, and got the urge to go to North Carolina, where she had heard of a commune that specialized in building straw and mud houses. Being interested in the environment, she packed her bags and was off on the next bus. She learned a lot about being self-sufficient during this time, and her experiences gave her an interest in environmental studies.

Leanne returned home and enrolled in a course in Peterborough to study trees. She loved the course, and made many like-minded friends. After graduation she was hired by the Credit Valley Conservation Authority as a field biologist. She loved her job. She bought a house in Orangeville and made the long, three-hour round trip to work and back daily.

She had a nice vegetable garden every year and some apple trees in her yard. Every Saturday during the summer, she worked at the local farmer's market. She renovated her whole house by herself, and took in boarders to help pay the mortgage. She was very happy in that house.

Leanne has a lot of patience. She taught a group of Girl Guides the merits of outdoor living. She took a creative writing course at the college and has written many interesting stories, complete with illustrations. She often goes hiking on the Bruce Trail. Every year she does the Christmas bird count with a group of friends. In her spare time, she catalogues mosses, rescues turtles, and maps frogs. You can sometimes find her mapping invasive species or planting native plants.

Recently she decided to apply for an environmental job in Kitchener with a private company. She got the job and really liked it, so she decided to move to Cambridge, where she now lives. She can work at home during days in the winter when the roads are snow-covered.

It can be difficult to be the sibling of a special needs child. Very often the time, resources, energy, and efforts of the parents are directed toward the child with needs and others can get lost in the shuffle. Leanne has managed to not only survive that, but to thrive, and to create a life for herself that brings her joy and peace. I'm so proud of the person she has become.

CHAPTER TWENTY

The Trip of a Lifetime

As the years went by, Darryl's liver deteriorated so much that he became very jaundiced. The doctors encouraged him to stay home from school and rest. He refused, as he was determined to get top marks in high school.

One day when he was around sixteen years old, I asked him, "If you could go anywhere in the world, where would it be?"

"England," he replied, a smile on his face. He never complained, no matter how sick he was. He always had a smile on his face. I decided I would find a way to make his dream happen.

My husband thought I was crazy to even consider taking him out of the country. He reminded me of the time we went to Disney World in Florida and how much trouble we'd had.

I contacted the hospital in Toronto and they set up a doctor in England for us to see in the event that Darryl became sick. We would take the portable pump and all the intravenous food with us. Every day's supplies would be individually packed in Ziploc bags. We decided we would rent a car and stay for twenty-one days.

Calea Pharmacy in Toronto agreed to pack Darryl's intravenous food in special crates with cool packs to keep the temperature steady during the eight-hour direct flight. Calea even hand-delivered all the needed supplies to the airport for us.

Leanne and Krystle came with us on the trip to help me carry the medical supplies. Each one of us packed only a backpack with clothes and toiletries for three weeks. I figured out that we would do the laundry each week and wear each clothing item three times.

We checked on the cheapest fares for both the plane and car rental through a well-known travel company based in Toronto. I contacted the medical desk at the airline we had booked with to make sure they were aware of all Darryl's medical needs. The food couldn't go in general baggage because it might freeze. Darryl would have to be hooked up to his machine, so the air space in his line was full of fluid due to the change in pressure while we were in the air. Everything was taken care of.

A week before we were due to depart, the phone rang. It was my representative at the travel agency. The airline had said, "We can't take you. You are too much of a risk. Your money will be refunded." And the lady hung up. I was in shock. Our bags were packed, the supplies had been bagged, and Darryl's food ordered. I couldn't believe it. How could they do this to us—to Darryl?

We were all heartbroken. I didn't know what to do, and Darryl was so disappointed. I had never seen him so sad—his dream was shattered. A friend told us about Helen Henderson, a writer for *The Toronto Star* who wrote a column once a week about disabled people. Maybe she could help? I contacted her, and she agreed to do a story. She said she would need a picture and she arranged for Glenn Ogilvie, a photographer with our local newspaper, *The Sarnia Observer*, to come to our house and take a picture of Darryl with his baseball bat and a puzzle he was working on. I explained the time constraints to Helen and she agreed it would be in Saturday's *Toronto Star*, but we couldn't read it before it was printed.

When the paper arrived, we grabbed it and opened it eagerly. The story about Darryl was on the front page of the "Life" section, and in colour! Air Canada saw the article and said they would take us on their plane and there would be no extra charge. It was amazing. The Air

Canada medical team contacted us and every detail was looked after. They put us in first class on a 747 jumbo jet. We had our own personal movie screen and a private flight attendant who served us all the food and drinks we could handle. We felt like royalty! We were each given a little pouch with toothpaste, toothbrush, facemask, socks, shaving cream, and razor. We watched the sun set and rise on the plane. It was beautiful. We thanked God for this blessing, and especially for Helen Henderson, who was His instrument. Unfortunately, she died a few years after our trip, and we never got to thank her in person.

LONDON, ENGLAND

When we arrived at Heathrow with five giant cases of food and one giant case of supplies, we were exhausted. We had travelled all night, and with the time change we were done in. We had brought three coolers on wheels, which we loaded with Darryl's intravenous food and bags of supplies. We had to leave several empty boxes with gel packs in them at the airport because there were a lot of extra ones after we put the food in the coolers.

We contemplated the car we had reserved and realized that all the stuff wouldn't fit in the Vauxhall Vectra. The nice lady at the Avis car rental counter upgraded us to a Peugeot 806 People Carrier—known to us as an automatic van. We laughed at the name, but it was perfect.

I had never driven on the other side of the road before, nor experienced having the steering wheel on the righthand side of the car. Getting out of the airport to our hotel was a scary experience.

In England they have a lot of roundabouts, making it faster to drive as long as you know where you are going. I was used to looking left to see oncoming traffic, so I had to consciously think *Look right!* at every roundabout. When we came to the first one, the smart people just stopped driving and let me pass. I'm surprised that we didn't get in an accident. Fortunately, the hotel was near the airport.

A few months before taking the children to England, Wayne and I had met a couple that lived in Northampton, just north of London. I had arranged for them to meet us at the hotel that afternoon after we had rested for a few hours. When I explained how much trouble I'd had driving to the hotel, our friend took me out for an hour's lesson. It was fabulous. After that, I wasn't scared to drive there anymore. We later visited them and they served us a delicious home-cooked meal.

Once we got out of London, it was easier to drive. The roads were narrow and the stone walls were intimidating, but I had helpers. Krystle sat in the back seat on the wall side, and she would say "Keep right" if I got too close. A good friend had given us a road map of Great Britain, and Leanne navigated from the passenger side front seat. Before leaving Canada, we had mapped out our route, which made travelling easier.

We stayed in Travelodges, since they could accommodate all four of us, and bought groceries at the store and ate breakfast in our room each morning. Sometimes we stayed in hostels. I found it nerve-wracking driving all day, but I enjoyed some wine, chocolate, and cheese at night.

We stopped in York and the kids did a "Ghost Walk." It was so much fun that they still talk about it to this day. While they were out, I did the laundry.

In Wales, we went to Caernarfon Castle. I was amazed that Darryl had enough energy to do the 565 stairs around the wall. We also toured Oxford University. I think we saw every church and castle there was to see. We got up to Glasgow to visit my cousin. I had never been to her place, and was intrigued that she had to put money in the gas meter every day to heat the house. The minimum age for car insurance in Great Britain was twenty-five, so I had to do all the driving.

We did so much travelling that some mornings the kids would say, "Can we just sleep in today?"

I wanted them to see everything, so I said, "No, just get up and have your shower and breakfast." They were always glad they did. In Wales, we picked strawberries and visited a sheep farmer. We saw how the border collie was being trained to herd the sheep. It was interesting because we had a border collie at home that used to herd our baby bunnies.

During the last day of the trip, Darryl had blood coming out of the tube from his stomach that drained off the bile. He was bringing up blood on the plane. I began to worry that he might not make it to

Toronto, and soon realized he was bleeding internally. He had to go to Toronto to the hospital for a while to get better. However, he said the trip had been worth it.

We had a great time, and I thanked God when we got home safely.

SCHOOL TRIP TO FRANCE

In Darryl's last year of high school, the school decided they would take a trip to France the following year, and he wanted to go. The school had never taken a trip overseas before. Darryl overcame so many medical challenges to do well in high school that the principal decided he would let him go on the trip to France even though that fall he was entering the University of Toronto. So in May 2005, after his first year of university, Darryl and I went on a school trip to Paris, Normandy, and Brittany. We stayed in small hotels that had been arranged beforehand. The two of us had our own room, and there was always a fridge to put Darryl's food in. The other kids shared four to a room. Since we had already done a twenty-one-day trip to England with all of Darryl's supplies, I knew we could do a nineteen-day trip to France.

Darryl and I left Canada a week earlier than the school because we wanted to rent a car and tour the south of France. He wanted to visit one of his friends from school that had a job taking care of children in a small town near Avignon. After landing in Paris, we went to Carcassonne, a medieval city, to see the famous castle. In Monaco, we visited the historic casino. Krystle joined us for the rest of the trip with the school. We picked her up at the Charles de Gaulle airport in Paris, stayed overnight in a hotel, and then met the rest of the kids at the airport the next day. We saw so many things and learned so much. It was truly a fantastic trip.

A lot of planning went into that trip regarding Darryl's intravenous food and supplies. We flew Air Canada again, and they helped us with all the details. Melodie at the medical desk in Montreal remembered us from the last trip, so it was easier this time. She was a wealth of information, and helped us to get through customs with all the medical supplies Darryl had to carry on board.

Travelling was a challenge every time, but it was always well worth the effort.

CHAPTER TWENTY-ONE

I Want to Be a Pharmacist

Darryl wanted to be a pharmacist. He took all the science and mathematics courses at high school, trying to meet every requirement for pharmacy. In no time at all, he became smarter than my husband and me. He was very competitive in school, and always wanted to get the top mark. When he graduated, he received about ten awards and scholarships. He also received a trophy for the highest overall average. His persistence and determination allowed him to overcome many obstacles. He was the class favourite amongst his peers.

We were so proud of him at the graduation ceremony, which was totally in French. My husband didn't understand much, but he could tell that Darryl was getting a lot of money and recognition. The cost for post-secondary education is daunting, and those monetary awards were greatly appreciated by Darryl—and us.

The only school in Ontario that gave a pharmacy degree was the University of Toronto, which was right across the road from the Toronto General Hospital. This was a blessing, as his care would be transferred from Sick Kids to Toronto General when he was nineteen. Darryl was accepted by the University of Toronto to do a Bachelor of Science in Human Biology. He had learned how to do all his dressings, run his intravenous food, and mix and run his drugs by himself, so I was confident with his decision to go to school so far away from us.

Darryl lived with a rare disease that required an enormous amount of effort, time, and maintenance, and the co-ordination of many life-sustaining activities, each designed to ensure his optimum health.

During his first year of university in 2004, aside from the usual pressures and stresses, Darryl had to ensure the ordering and delivery of all his medical supplies on a weekly basis. He had a central line break that required surgery, several obstructions in his bowel, and a g-tube break that required hospitalization. These unforeseen challenges directly affected his academic work. However, despite all these setbacks, eighteen-year-old Darryl successfully completed his first year of full-time studies at the University of Toronto.

At least one year of undergrad was required before students could apply to get into the pharmacy program. A few thousand students applied for 250 places, and Darryl didn't get in. He completed his second year in science and applied again. This time he was accepted. When he was admitted to the pharmacy program, he was still sick, but he managed to get good marks. Mentally he was sound, but physically he was a mess. I wondered how he kept going.

Darryl had worked extremely hard, and we thanked God for how far he had come. It was tiring for him to walk too far, so being on campus worked well. He didn't need to buy the meal plan because he didn't eat. He was totally fed by intravenous. We had to get special permission to have him exempt from the meal plan, and for him to have a thirteen-cubic-foot fridge in his room. His closet was full of medical supplies rather than clothes.

Darryl made friends easily and really enjoyed being in residence. He had taken his expensive bike with him, and rode it to school. One day he chained it up outside the pharmacy building, and when he came out someone had stolen it. He was devastated. He was discovering the pitfalls of living in a big city.

His first placement was at Princess Margaret Hospital on the oncology ward. It really opened his eyes to the effects of cancer drugs. He was part of a team of doctors and pharmacists looking after a certain number of patients. On Fridays, they would send people home if the drugs weren't working.

"Does that mean they're fine?" I asked him.

He replied, "No, we are sending them home to die." It must have been so hard on him, knowing he was at death's door too. He was quite jaundiced because only about twenty percent of his liver worked.

Darryl grew sicker by the day. His doctors couldn't understand how he was still walking around. I offered to donate part of my liver and went through all the necessary tests, but he was put on the multi-organ donor list in October of 2005. The doctors agreed that a multi-organ transplant was the only solution, although even that offered only a fifty percent chance of survival. This decision was made because if he only got a liver from me, for example, the TPN would eventually destroy it. He needed a liver, large and small bowel, stomach and pancreas.

The transplant doctor said he had a good chance of getting the organs because he needed so many. They had done a four-organ transplant on a young boy a few months before, and he was still alive. That was comforting. His story had been on the front page of the *Toronto Star*, so I felt hopeful. The transplant was Darryl's only chance of survival.

It took every ounce of faith that we were doing the right thing, as the thought of losing our only son kept me awake at night. He was so courageous and optimistic. Darryl and I were both given pagers so that the hospital could contact us any time, day or night, if they had a donor. We waited.

I prayed that the pager would go off, but lived in fear of the moment that it would.

CHAPTER TWENTY-TWO

The Transplant

The call came at the end of November 2006, when Darryl had a few exams left in his first term. He was twenty years old. Wayne and I alternated between fear and elation as we threw a few things in a suitcase and drove to the hospital in Toronto. Good thing there was hardly any traffic, as we were in a big hurry to get there (to put it mildly).

As an adult, Darryl had to make the decision whether or not to have the surgery, but he didn't hesitate, knowing this was his only chance of survival. He went into surgery at 10:00 in the morning, and came out at 11:00 that night. A team of specialists had worked on him all day: the liver doctor, the bowel doctor, the urology team, the transplant surgeon, and all the nurses.

Staying in the waiting room with all the other parents was excruciatingly difficult. It was hard to concentrate on anything constructive like reading or sewing. There was a television in the room, but it had the news on most of the time—usually murders and robberies. Depressing. Every time a doctor would enter the room, all eyes were on him. Hopes were dashed when your name wasn't called. Gradually people left and we remained—waiting.

Finally, the transplant doctor came in and called our name. We jumped up immediately. He came right over and told us Darryl was in recovery and heavily sedated. He told us a nurse would come out from time to time and give us reports on how he was doing. If he was stable, he would be moved up to the ward later and we'd be allowed to see him. We were instructed to wait in the tenth floor waiting room.

It was horrifying to see him when he was first brought to the Intensive Care Unit for post-op transplant patients. He had been cut from one end to the other, and had at least twelve intravenous lines going into all parts of his body. A bag at the side of the bed collected his urine. A breathing tube was taped to his face. The tube was removed a few days later once he was breathing on his own.

Darryl's private room was right beside the nurse's station on the acute transplant floor. There were so many intravenous pumps in the room that there was hardly room for us. A nurse sat at the end of his bed, watching him and all the machines. He was so puffy that we hardly recognized him. The surgeon told us that if he survived the next twenty-four critical hours, he might live. We prayed hard that he would recover, and he made it through the night—hallelujah!

As Darryl lay in the hospital bed near death after his transplant, I thought about all the things that had worried me the day before. I was realizing they were trivial. All that mattered was that he got better.

I stayed beside my son's bed for three days and nights. Everyone we knew, and even people we didn't know who lived as far away as Saskatchewan, were praying that he would survive and be healthy. On the fourth day, the drugs were making him hallucinate. He didn't know who I was and he yelled at me to leave, to get out. It felt like a knife through my heart. Darryl thought the doctors were the police, and ordered them out too. He was even swearing, which was totally out of character for him.

I ran out of the room crying. The nurse followed me and assured me that it was the drugs and that he didn't know what he was saying. She encouraged me to come back, but I couldn't. Wayne stayed with him until the next day. I was crushed. I cried most of the night thinking he might not survive and I wouldn't be there.

BUMPS IN THE ROAD

Over the next two weeks, Darryl had to return to the operating table more than once for complications that needed to be fixed. I remember one time specifically. When I entered Darryl's room, I always looked at his incision to see how it was healing. Staples held his skin together from his breast bone all the way down past his belly button. That day, green fluid poured out of all the spaces between the staples and you could see all the tissue underneath. Thinking back, it looked like a hot dog that had split open after being cooked. When was the last time the nurses had checked on him?

I frantically ran to the nurses' station and told them what I had found, and the nurse paged the doctor on call. When the doctor arrived, he said that there was a leak somewhere and bile was oozing out of his incision. They would have to open Darryl back up again, locate and fix the leak, then staple him up again. He was in surgery for several hours that day.

Another incident happened one night around 10:30 p.m. while I was sitting with him. I was alone as Wayne had gone back home to look after the other children and to return to work. Darryl started having trouble breathing, so I ran to tell the nurse, who quickly paged the doctor on call. A resident doctor came and said Darryl's lung had collapsed.

The staff doctors worked during the day and the residents worked at night. I was always leery when the residents were in charge, because they didn't have as much experience as the staff doctors. Since Darryl's case was rare, I was hesitant to follow the residents' decisions in caring for him, and I always made them call the staff doctor so he could agree with their diagnosis and procedures.

This time, the resident came back from the call and said Darryl needed to have a chest tube put in immediately to drain the fluid that had accumulated in his left lung. He said there wasn't enough time to take him to the operating room and that he would have to insert it right then and there. Darryl wasn't even sedated when the doctor pushed a long tube, half an inch wide, into the space between his two ribs, guided only by touch. He screamed in agony. I was right outside the room with just a curtain between us. It was all I could do to stay in the chair and not run right in.

When I finally saw Darryl, he had a large tube taped to his chest that drained yellowish fluid into a bucket at the side of his bed. A little blood from the incision had leaked into the tube as well. Darryl breathed a little easier now. The tube was left in for a few days to make sure all the fluid had drained off his lung. I felt sorry for him. Hadn't he endured enough?

The physiotherapist got Darryl up walking within a few days. I thought it was too soon, but I'm like a mother bear with her cub. The first day he walked to the door. The next day he made it down the hall a little. He leaned on a tall walker with a nurse on each side of him while I pushed the intravenous pumps behind. His urine bag had been hung on the pump. Darryl was on a lot of intravenous medications. Everyone who entered his room had to put on a gown and mask, and we had to wear rubber gloves if we wanted to touch him. His immunity was suppressed and he could very easily pick up germs that might kill him.

As a precaution, the doctor put him on medication to treat meningitis. We believe this was because the donor had died of it, although the doctors didn't confirm our suspicions. In the *Toronto Star*, there had been an article about a young man who had contracted meningitis and died the Sunday night before Darryl's transplant. I thought it was too much of a coincidence that Darryl would have to take medication to treat meningitis for a month after his transplant if that young boy wasn't his donor. I wrote a letter to his mother thanking her for her unselfish gift to us that had enabled Darryl to live. In the letter, I called Darryl "our child" because he carried her son's organs too. I write her every year to make sure she knows her son's life continues in Darryl.

Christmas arrived, and Darryl was doing well. He was a month post-transplant. All our family gathered in his room to celebrate, and the nurse took our picture. A giant box came from Wayne's workplace with presents for all. A seven-course Christmas dinner was delivered by the Royal York Hotel—the swankiest hotel in Toronto. Krystle's company,

Parrish and Heimbecker, had sent it. Darryl couldn't eat, but the rest of us enjoyed ourselves. Things were looking up, and we thanked God for this miracle.

The other young boy who'd had a four-organ transplant a few months earlier came to our room, and we took pictures of "the boys." His mom brought a big gift-wrapped box filled with all sorts of neat things for Darryl. The other boy went home in January. Sadly, he had a few complications and died in June on Father's Day. It was also his father's birthday that day, so it was especially tragic.

Darryl went home near the end of January, in time to celebrate his twenty-first birthday. However, it wasn't very long before he was back on the ward with a virus. The donor had carried a virus called cytomegalovirus (cmv) and it had been passed on to Darryl. He experienced flu-like symptoms for the next two years periodically as a result of the virus, but he always recovered.

I was working at the Marriott Reservation Centre, but during the time I was in Toronto, I had to take a leave of absence. However, Marriott gave me free lodging at the downtown hotels, as well as some near the Toronto airport. They also gave me food. It was amazing to have a beautiful place to stay and to be fed too. I thanked God for the generosity of my employer.

DARRYL'S NEW ORGANS

Darryl had received a complete bowel (small and large intestine), a stomach, a pancreas, and a liver all from one donor. It was a very good match. They had to remove Darryl's spleen because they couldn't fit all the organs into Darryl's body as the donor had been bigger than him. They left Darryl's pancreas in, so he actually has two of them now.

He had to have an ileostomy (a surgical procedure to divert part of the bowel to an opening in the abdominal wall) to drain his bowel while the organs healed inside. The ileostomy drained the bowel contents into a bag that was taped to Darryl's side. The bag had to be drained daily, and the seal replaced every few days. Sometimes it would leak or fall off completely, and the liquid would get all over the bedsheets or his clothes. It was to be removed after about six months, but after a year and a half he still had it. One day Darryl decided it finally needed to be removed, and he discussed this with the transplant doctor at his next visit. The doctor agreed, and it was removed and the bowel joined successfully.

Darryl was also given a gastrostomy tube (g-tube) that went directly into his stomach to feed him liquid food that wouldn't damage his liver. He had to run the pump all night to get enough calories, and sometimes the tube would break or get plugged and need to be replaced.

TRANSITION TO REALITY

In August, before Darryl went back to university, Krystle got married. It was our first wedding and we were all very excited. Darryl was nine months post-transplant at this point, and he was well enough to attend. He was all dressed up in a new suit. At one point, he started dancing with Krystle. Everyone on the dance floor stopped in their tracks, made a circle around them, and started clapping. It was a surreal moment for our family. I began to cry, and within a few minutes almost everyone was crying or had tears in their eyes.

After the transplant, Darryl could eat food, but not enough to survive on. He hadn't eaten for over twenty years, so it was a strange sensation for him. He tried all sorts of foods. He didn't like the texture of mashed potatoes. When we had green beans one night, he said, "Why do people eat these?" It was funny—I still laugh.

Darryl joined us the first Thanksgiving after his transplant, and he had some comical mishaps. He didn't know which hand to hold his fork in, and he didn't know how to cut the meat. That skill was so basic for us that we forgot how foreign it would be for Darryl. One day he took a knife out of the drawer to cut some meat. It didn't have a serrated edge, and he said, "Why do they make these?" He didn't realize it was a butter knife.

Eventually all the tubes were taken out, and he began to eat everything. He still has trouble gaining weight, but he manages. Now he only takes a daily anti-rejection drug and acid inhibitor. He likes to go to the gym every other day to keep in shape. Every four months he needs his throat stretched so he can eat, which involves inserting a long plastic tube about an inch thick down his throat while he is partially sedated.

There is a stricture in his esophagus about twelve inches down his throat that prevents food from moving through easily, so this is necessary. Once a year during this procedure, a bowel biopsy is performed to check for organ rejection.

Darryl didn't complete his first year of pharmacy before the transplant, but the school held his spot until the following September (2007). Ten months post-transplant, Darryl returned to school to complete his Bachelor of Pharmacy degree—a little too soon in my mind, but he was determined to get it done. He is tenacious and driven. It was a four-year program and he lived in residence right beside the hospital so when he needed tests or was sick he could just walk over. He was close to the pharmacy building as well. This made me feel more at ease.

Darryl decided he would prefer to work at a pharmacy, not a hospital. After graduation, he was required to do a four-month placement in Toronto. He rented a small room in Leslieville in Toronto while he worked at a local Shoppers Drug Mart. We bought him a cheaper bicycle this time that he stored inside his apartment. When he rode it to work, he brought it into the store.

Darryl finished his placement, then wrote his final exams in Kingston and passed. I went out and bought a new outfit in anticipation of the day of his graduation in June 2011 at the University of Toronto. It was a bright sunny day and we were all excited. We reserved a hotel in Toronto and a special table at an elegant restaurant. We were so proud when he walked across the stage. He had overcome countless obstacles just to survive. He had worked so hard for so long, and finally he had accomplished his goal of being a pharmacist.

The class started out with two hundred and fifty students and ended up with just over one hundred graduates. We took pictures of Darryl in his robes with the biggest smile I have ever seen on his face. There was a big tent set up where we could buy a frame for his degree and picture.

When Darryl graduated from university, we had a big party at our house. Our pediatrician and his wife were invited. I felt he'd helped me keep Darryl alive all these years. All the people who had been praying for Darryl came to our house, and all his friends and ours gathered to rejoice in Darryl's accomplishments. People brought gifts and cards. Food was shared, stories were told, and we thanked God.

Darryl was fortunate to get a job at a local Shoppers Drug Mart in Sarnia so he could live at home and save money for a house. He was immune suppressed and often got colds and flu from the sick people coming in for prescriptions. Many of them were grumpy, but he learned how to deal with difficult customers. He has the gift of never getting angry or becoming short with people. He is fluent in French and sometimes gets to assist French people when they come into the store. Darryl was on a lot of drugs when he was younger, so he knows how that feels, and he can explain firsthand what side effects could arise.

After a year of living with us and working at the local pharmacy, Darryl moved out and into his own apartment overlooking the Bluewater Bridge. He has done extremely well and we are proud of him. We thank God, and know without a doubt that He was surely in charge.

BREATHING EASIER

Wayne retired in 2012 after forty years of working at New Life Mills. He wanted to put all the children through university and make sure they were well on their way before he retired. He accomplished that goal and now he can relax.

Wayne has taken care of our family through thick and thin. We were married in 1977 and celebrated our forty-second wedding anniversary this past May. In all that time, I have never heard Wayne complain about one thing. He missed only a few days of work in forty years. I couldn't have chosen a better man. I thanked God for that gift, too.

A poem written by the late Erma Bombeck entitled "The Special Mother" gives me comfort. As Bombeck notes, many disabled babies are born to women each year. She believes that God chooses who will give birth to a less than perfect baby. He chooses mothers who are happy, independent, and a little bit selfish—after all, Bombeck writes, "If she can't separate herself from the child occasionally, she'll never survive." Even if they don't believe in Him, He stays by their side to give them patience and guide them in doing His work—"She will never be alone.

I will be at her side every minute of every day of her life because she is doing my work as surely as she is here by my side."[2]

Some say it was the doctors who saved Darryl. I believe it was God performing a miracle through the skilled hands of doctors and nurses. God does perform miracles today and, in our son, we have absolutely witnessed one.

---

[2] Erma Bombeck, *Motherhood: The Second Oldest Profession* (New York: McGraw-Hill, 1983), pp. 70–72.

Chapter Twenty-Three

Where Are We Now?

At church recently, our pastor talked about finding purpose in life. He asked, "Why are you here?" He said that God will give us everything we need to accomplish the goals He has for us, even if those goals seem inconceivable. We must trust God to bring us everything we need, not everything we want. Sometimes God says "no" to our requests. I believe God wanted me to write this book to encourage other moms going through difficult times with their children. He wants us to pray about everything we need, even if it seems impossible in our minds.

While working at Shoppers Drug Mart, Darryl met Jamie. They got to know each other and starting going out. Jamie had a young daughter, Olivia, from a previous relationship. Darryl loved her too. After a year of dating, Darryl proposed. They set the date for the wedding.

My best friend hosted a bridal shower for Jamie. Over the years we had gotten to know our pediatrician's wife very well, and she came to the shower. The secretary from Darryl's school came too because I had talked to her many times when Darryl got sick at school. He would go to the nurse's office right beside the secretary and wait to be picked up. She admired his stamina.

The shower gave me a chance to get to know the bridesmaids, Jamie's mom, and Jamie's aunts. It gave Jamie a chance to meet my closest friends and her soon to be sisters-in-law—Heather and Krystle. Krystle's daughter Amber is the same age as Olivia, and they hit it off right away.

The wedding day was perfect—not a cloud in the sky. The couple had their pictures done in Canatara Park in Sarnia. Darryl embraced Olivia as if she were his own. We are so happy to have Jamie and Olivia as part of our family. We can see how happy they have made Darryl, and that pleases us to no end.

In 2015, Darryl got a golden retriever puppy, and it was like it was his baby. He took really good care of him, training Winston every second. We call him our "grandpuppy." He is a good dog. I knew at that moment that if Darryl did have a child, he would be a good, loving father. After all, he's had a good role model with his own dad.

November 27, 2016 was a particularly special day for our family. It marked the tenth anniversary of Darryl's transplant. Wow! We were elated that he was doing so well. We could never have envisioned that he would marry, get a job, and own a house.

We had another big party to celebrate with all his friends and all the people who had prayed for him and supported us over the years. Our pediatrician again came with his wife. I thanked him for all the years he had cared for our family. It was great to see Darryl behave as a completely normal adult talking to other adults as if nothing tragic had ever happened.

Darryl trained at the gym a few summers ago for a five-kilometre warrior dash with Jamie. He ran through the mud, climbed obstacles, swam through very cold water and jumped over fire. He posted his picture on Facebook all covered in mud and smiling. He said it was tough, but he can't wait until another one comes along to enter again. He continually surprises me with his accomplishments.

Sometimes when he is working at the pharmacy, a lady will come in and say, "My knees are sore." Darryl gets a puzzled look on his face as he wonders what she means. Does she have arthritis? He has no clue who this lady is or what she expects him to do. Then she says, "I prayed for you for twenty years." A smile appears on his face and he realizes that she must be a friend of mine. Prayer works. God heals even today.

Darryl was a guest with Anna Jaworski on her radio program "Heart to Heart with Anna." On this particular series, she was interviewing people who have had transplants. Anna asked Darryl questions about what it was like growing up with three sisters, being tethered to an intravenous machine for fourteen or more hours per day, and his transplant journey. The audio interview is available online for you to listen to.[3]

DARRYL IN HIS OWN WORDS

Here is a Facebook post written by Darryl on his thirty-second birthday in 2018:

Today is my thirty-second birthday.

I have a beautiful wife, two amazing children, a happy golden retriever and a fantastic career that allows me to help people on a daily basis. From the outside looking in one might think I have it all.

But life wasn't always this way. There were days when I fell asleep not knowing if I would wake up the next morning. There was more than one occasion where my parents had to watch me wheeled away on a stretcher not knowing if they would ever speak to me again. I underwent countless surgical procedures that could have easily killed me. There were days and weeks of unimaginable pain, and multiple months spent in the hospital.

I was born with a medical condition called gastrointestinal pseudo-obstruction and hollow visceral myopathy. My stomach could not absorb nutrients and my intestinal tract was non-functional. The only solution at the time was to go on total parenteral nutrition, which means I was fed by IV tubing

---

[3] Darryl and Anna's interview can be accessed at https://www.blogtalkradio.com/hearttoheartwithanna/2018/07/24/multiple-organ-transplant-due-to-gastric-intestinal-pseudo-obstruction.

overnight, every night, for twenty years. The doctors had no solution, no cure, and the only plan was to keep me alive long enough that medical advances would allow for an organ transplant. And they did; for twenty years I lived this way. My family did the best they could to give me a normal upbringing. I went to school, played baseball, and lived as normal a life as I could. I went off to university and studied as hard as I could. And then at the age of nineteen, with my health deteriorating, I was placed on the transplant list. The IV feeds were slowly destroying my liver, and a transplant was the only option. But replacing a liver alone would not have been a permanent solution. They needed to replace the stomach, the liver, and the entire intestinal tract. And then in November of 2006, I got a call at 2 a.m.

They had the organs. All of them from one person.

This most generous, selfless act from one very special person gave me a shot at a new life. A normal life. No IV feeds, no more fatigue, and no more being stuck to an IV pole in my room for fourteen hours a night. The recovery was not easy, and I still spent multiple months in the hospital after the transplant. I had to choose to remain positive even when things seemed bleakest. I made it out, and a whole new chapter of my life could begin. The scars you see on my body I wear with pride, as they are a reminder of a selfless young man who had to lose his life in order for me to live mine.

Fast forward to today, and my son Owen is beginning to display symptoms of the same debilitating condition. What I hope for Owen is that he does not have this condition, or at the very least that it is a more mild presentation. I hope he lives his life happy and healthy and without a care in the world.

But even if he is healthy, there will always be people like me who need organ transplants. If my story can help change even one person's mind, to cause someone to think about becoming an organ donor, then that would be the best birthday present I could ever ask for. If you have any questions about the process I am happy to answer them. Or visit beadonor.ca.

There have been a lot of replies to Darryl's Facebook post from his friends, and also from people he does not know. Here is one from Scott, a classmate, that gave me insight into Darryl's daily life.

For ten of these years we were in grade school together and I had the pleasure of being in class, sometimes seated right next to this amazing guy. He's by far the strongest, most resilient, forward-thinking person that I know. I mean, he would go through bouts of jaundice and liver failure like we get colds and he'd still show up to gym class.

Darryl, just as he says in his story, was always fed by IV during the night, so this meant that at school, during lunch, he couldn't physically eat anything with us, his classmates. There were a couple of times he had procedures done that would allow him to eat, and this was exciting for everyone in class. We'd take turns asking him to eat something with us, it was awesome. Darryl was eating with us! This was short lived and after a couple of days he would be back to his "normal" and wasn't able to eat anything. His "normal" was everyone else's worst nightmare and through everything he's kept his head up high and hasn't lost his smile.

Darryl, to see you turn thirty-two is inspiring and you know what, having known you for so long, I'm not surprised you made it. I hope you have an amazing birthday with your beautiful family, you deserve it!! Without an organ donor his story may have turned out different.

Another comment came from a lady who had lost her husband a year earlier and had donated all his organs. She was very glad to understand how the recipient felt. A young mom also said she had a son who was awaiting all the same organs that Darryl had received. Her son too was on TPN and it was killing his liver. I empathized with her and responded on Facebook to never give up hope. I told her I would pray for her son. Darryl's post encouraged her to never give up as well.

His story was shared over 350 times and 150 people made comments, some of whom he didn't know. A lot of people signed up to be organ donors. Darryl was quite humbled by all the responses.

In November 2019, on the thirteenth anniversary of his transplant, Darryl posted the following message on social media.

This will be a lengthy post but it can be summarized simply as: Please consider organ donation, I would not be here today without a wonderful, selfless donor. (https://www.beadonor.ca/)

People often ask me how my day is going. "How are you doing," "How are things," etc. My default answer is always "good." Things are good, my life is good, and work is good. It's a short answer, an easy answer, and technically true

Of course, like all of us, I have some days that are "more" good, and some days that are "less" good. But when I look to the past, and then look at how my life is now, it's clear that there are no "bad" days.

Today marks the thirteenth anniversary of my multi-organ transplant. On November 27, 2006 I received a new liver, bowel, stomach, and pancreas. For many, thirteen is an unlucky number. For me, it is a symbol of hope.

We often hear about people on their deathbed who wish they could have one more day. We hear stories of widows and orphans whose only wish is for one more day with the one that they have lost.

Every single day since that transplant is my "one more day." Each and every day that I wake up, that I can breathe is a gift. I've come closer to death than anyone should ever have to get, and I do my best to be mindful of that as I go about daily routines.

There are things I have done that I thought would never be possible for me.

I eat now, every day. This seems like a funny thing to say, but I spent the first twenty years of my life almost never eating.

All of my nutrition came by intravenous TPN and the muscles in my throat atrophied from lack of use. Now there are some days it seems like all I do is eat. I can vividly remember a time as a child when my mom asked me if I could have one wish, anything, what it would be. And I said it would be to eat. Just to be able to eat. I didn't wish to be 100% healthy, I didn't wish to not have all of my lines, all of the tubes coming out of me. All I wanted was just to be able to eat. To me, that was the ultimate goal. If I could just eat, then I would be OK. I would be "normal." And now, I can eat. I have since realized that there is no "normal" and we are all made to be different.

I was able to finish my university degree, pass all the required pharmacy exams, and now I get to go to work every day and make a tangible difference in the life of my pharmacy patients. I was able to work in retail pharmacy for eight years and saw the direct impact I was having on families and caregivers every day. Now I work in long-term care, and my goal every day is to help my patients fully enjoy the late stages of their lives. I also make it possible for the families of these patients to have that one more day with their loved ones. It's not always an easy job, but I truly believe it is always making a difference.

I was able to meet my wife, who is without question the best thing that has ever happened to me. Without her I would probably have remained the quiet, introverted, shy person I had always been. She has done more than anyone to really help me grow as a person. She introduced me to fitness and showed me what is really possible. She showed me that crawling through mud, jumping over fire, and swimming in freezing cold water were not things one should avoid; but "obstacles" to attack just to prove you can.

I can remember in the weeks post-transplant barely having the strength to lift my arms. Walking a few steps in my room with a walker felt like a marathon. I couldn't breathe, I couldn't think. But soon I was walking down the hallway. And then two hallways. And then around the whole unit. Pretty soon I didn't need the walker at all. My parents never took it easy on me, ever. Throughout my entire life they made sure I always put in the effort they knew I was capable of. When I was younger I had all the same chores as my siblings; I had to put out the garbage, I had to walk the dog, and I had to clean the house. This continued post-transplant. My dad wouldn't let me just point at a cup of water. He made me use my voice, however weak it was. He made me reach for paper if I wanted to write a note. He could just as easily have done everything for me. But this would only have delayed my recovery—he knew it would not help. I might not have enjoyed it at the time, but I know now just how necessary that was.

Because of this, I hit a personal milestone today of deadlifting three hundred pounds. I've always seen myself as small, short, and weak. But the stories we tell ourselves are not always true. We are capable of far more than we can imagine.

I have been able to travel without boundaries, without planning, without worrying about all the things that could go wrong. I've been to a dozen US states, Scotland, England, Disney World, and camping in Algonquin Park. And all with very minimal planning. Before the transplant my parents made sure I was able to see the world, but it would take upwards of a year to plan a two week vacation. Every detail was considered. There were backup plans, and backups for the backups. Every single thing that could possibly go wrong had to be imagined, and then planned for. There was no "let's just drive and see where we end up." Most people have an emergency kit in their car that has a small first aid kit, maybe a blanket, and a battery booster if you want to get really fancy. Our emergency kit more closely resembled the inside of an ambulance. To say that my mom had thought of everything would be the understatement of the decade.

Earlier this year, as many of you know, my son Owen got very sick, very fast. He was rushed to London, was in the ICU for two weeks, and eventually had his entire small bowel removed. He spent just over two months in the hospital, half in London, and half in Toronto. He now requires TPN for all of his nutrition and will need a transplant at some point. There is no question of if, only when. The five year survival rate for the transplant he will require is still only 50%. This is not significantly better than it was when I had my transplant thirteen years ago. Luckily, he is currently doing as well as can be expected. He is young enough that he doesn't remember any different way of life, and has not yet started asking many questions about his condition. He just takes everything in stride. He does have his mother's temper, but that's a different discussion altogether. His sister Olivia has been a source of strength and kindness in his life. No matter how angry he gets, no matter the tantrums, no matter if he throws things at her or kicks her, she is always there for him. Looking after him and keeping him out of trouble.

His illness has really given me a much better insight into the challenge that my parents had when I was growing up. The constant stress and worry of what might go wrong. The long days at hospital appointments. The constant phone calls trying to figure out who to talk to in what department. I've spent more hours than I care to remember on the phone with my drug plan trying to figure out what, if anything they will cover of Owen's supplies. There are days when I just feel like throwing my phone across the room because it seems like nobody knows what they are doing. But I get it: his is a complicated case. He's not in the flowchart; there is no manual for his circumstances.

This is getting long so I will just end with a quote which has helped me over the past thirteen years.

"I judge you unfortunate because you have never lived through misfortune. You have passed through life without an opponent—no one can ever know what you are capable of, not even you" (Seneca).

And finally a reminder that organ donation is the ultimate gift. We have the power within us to give a new life to another human. It is impossible to overstate the impact that organ donation can have on the life of the recipient and their friends and family.

CHAPTER TWENTY-FOUR

Owen

Darryl wanted children of his own. He and his wife had trouble conceiving, but with a little help from science, they were able to have a little boy, Owen, in August 2016. The best part is that he lives only five minutes away from us. Darryl was the first Wallis boy in our family in over thirty years. Kevin, Wayne's younger brother, had a son a few months after Darryl. Owen is the third boy in all those years, and we are so proud and happy.

When Darryl's little boy Owen was around five months old, I felt something wasn't right with him. His stools were not formed, and he had a lot of pain and strain passing them. He went through a lot of diapers each day. He always woke up in the night and he usually had soiled his diaper. His stomach was big and hard, as though it was full of gas. Was history repeating itself?

Darryl took him to a specialist an hour from his house and the doctor said that he couldn't digest the formula. The doctor recommended an easily-digested formula and thought that Owen would outgrow the problem. However, Darryl took him back at seven months because he was vomiting a lot. He wasn't gaining weight. The doctor said Owen was fine and to wait until he was a year old because they didn't do any tests on babies that young.

I knew that they did tests on children under a year of age, but he was Darryl and Jamie's son and they had to make the decisions for his care. At around sixteen months, Owen stopped gaining weight. His tummy was distended, and he was vomiting even more often than before—mostly green bile. He was a good eater, but had trouble absorbing the nutrients. He was happy and played well with his toys unless he had pains in his tummy. It was easy to tell when that happened, because he would just stand still and start to cry. We all felt sorry for him, but we didn't know what to do about it.

In the meantime, Darryl and Jamie had considered having more children. Darryl wanted to make sure nothing would be passed on to future children, so he had some genetic testing done in 2017. Darryl's transplant doctor had contacted him saying that there had been some progress in identifying the gene causing visceral myopathy and Darryl could be tested.

The test showed that Darryl had one mutated gene, MYH11, which in mice has been shown to cause problems with motility and smooth muscle. The geneticist suggested that Wayne and I be tested to see if we were carriers of the mutated gene. The results showed we weren't carriers. The doctors said that what Darryl had was a new disease. There was only one other documented case with this mutated gene—a six-month-old baby. That baby was a little different because both parents carried the mutated gene.

Owen also had genetic testing done, and the results showed that he too was carrying the mutated MYH11 gene. Any other children that Jamie and Darryl had would also have a fifty percent chance of being born with this gene mutation. We were devastated to hear this. It was our worst nightmare.

Owen was taken to the hospital recently to undergo some nuclear medicine tests to show the motility of his digestive tract. This specialized test revealed that Owen's motility in his bowel is slower than normal. Motility is the contraction of the muscles that mix and propel food through the gastro-intestinal (GI) tract. The doctors have decided to start him on a drug to increase the time it takes for the food to pass through his intestines. The geneticist did tell us that Darryl can pass this motility problem on to Owen in a milder form.

Owen has been diagnosed with Hollow Viceral Myopathy, which essentially means the muscles and nerves don't move food through his digestive tract very quickly. We hope this drug will alleviate some of the discomfort he is having and will allow him to absorb more nutrients faster and start gaining weight. He hasn't gained much weight for at least six months. The gene mutation that Darryl and Owen have has been linked to aortic aneurysms, but thankfully all of Darryl's echocardiograms have been normal. Owen will have to have this monitored every two years.

In February 2019, after weeks of vomiting and having a large distended stomach, our two-and-a-half-year-old grandson was taken to the London hospital in serious condition. Circulation was cut off to his legs due to the fluid in his abdomen, and he was in severe pain. Twenty-two health care professionals worked tirelessly trying to relieve the pressure in his abdomen. Eventually, emergency surgery was performed where his abdomen was cut open to release the fluid. He was intubated and sedated for days. His abdomen could not be closed until all the fluid was drained off. The doctors went in three different times to check the condition of the small intestine, which was very inflamed. The final time, the small intestine had died, so they took it out and closed the incision. The top part of Owen's duodenum and his large intestine were sewn up. A g-tube was inserted to drain his stomach, and an indwelling catheter collected his urine in a large bag at the bedside.

Darryl is very capable of taking care of Owen's medical needs, and understands firsthand how he is feeling. Owen has a central line, g-tube, and colostomy, just like Darryl had. We are hopeful that Owen will have a successful transplant in the future. Right now, he is a happy three-year-old enjoying the only life he knows with two amazing parents who are caring for him day and night.

Owen is now on intravenous feeding (TPN), just like Darryl was, although the formula is less toxic to his liver. Owen has the same doctor as Darryl had at Sick Kids in Toronto, and spends a lot of time on the same ward.

His duodenum was reattached to his large intestine in May 2019, and a colostomy was performed to drain his bowel. He can eat food, but liquids are restricted.

Owen has had many tests to get him ready to be listed for a transplant of his small intestine, colon, pancreas, and perhaps a liver.

Even though the situation seems dire, I feel a peace that Owen will be fine and Darryl and Jamie will be able to cope with his medical needs. My faith has not wavered.

God is good. We have to trust that Owen will be fine. With God all things are possible. God is control of everything, and God has a purpose for each of us to fulfil. I had to trust God to take care of Darryl; I am now trusting God to take care of Owen and to give Darryl and Jamie the strength to cope.

When I look at Darryl's wife Jamie, I see myself as a young mom. She knows nothing about all the medical terms and tests. She wonders what Owen's life will be like. However, she is coping well with her "new normal." She has learned how to do all the medical procedures necessary to keep Owen healthy.

I know exactly how she feels. If I hadn't had the experience with the doctors, nurses, and community agencies when Heather was born, I wouldn't have been able to cope when Darryl came along. I had to trust God continually and pray without ceasing just to get through each day. Sometimes it was moment by moment. What really helped me were the times my girlfriends would say when we were together, "Let's pray right now." Bowing their heads on the spot, they would pray for me and my family. I felt a great calm come over me. I could feel God in our midst.

Jamie and Darryl have Facebook with which to share their story and have people pray for them instantly. Networking is much easier.

Today our kids are making their own family traditions. Krystle got married and takes her three children to Algonquin Park each summer. She celebrates Easter with her family and in-laws on Good Friday, then comes to our house for Easter Sunday. Leanne usually has a barbeque on Father's Day for the whole family. Krystle and Darryl have their own Christmas celebrations with their families in the morning, and then come to our house for the big get-together in the afternoon.

God had a plan for my life and for the lives of every member of my family. I hope and pray the goals He has for each one of us have been or will be met. I know now that they can be, with God's help. Acts 13:36 says that David fulfilled the purpose God had for him in his life, and then he died. My hope and prayer is that the same can be said of me, and of Wayne, Leanne, Heather, Krystle, and Darryl.

And I believe with all my heart that, whatever challenges you face in life, Christ will give you the strength to face and overcome them all, and you will be able to fulfil the purpose that God has for your life. I challenge you to trust God to see you through these challenges.

GLOSSARY

Central venous catheter (CVC): "…a thin, flexible tube (**catheter**) that is placed into a large vein above the heart. It may be inserted through a vein in the neck, chest, or arm. It's also called a **central venous line** or **central line**."[4]

Cerebral shunts: "….commonly used to treat **hydrocephalus**, the swelling of the brain due to excess buildup of cerebrospinal fluid (CSF). If left unchecked, the cerebrospinal fluid can build up, leading to an increase in intracranial pressure (ICP) which can lead to intracranial hematoma, cerebral edema, crushed brain tissue or herniation. The cerebral shunt can be used to alleviate or prevent these problems in patients who suffer from hydrocephalus or other related diseases. Shunts can come in a variety of forms but most of them consist of a valve housing connected to a catheter, the end of which is usually placed in the peritoneal cavity."[5]

---

[4] "Central Venous Catheter," Cancer.ca (https://www.cancer.ca/en/cancer-information/diagnosis-and-treatment/tests-and-procedures/central-venous-catheter/?region=on)
[5] "Cerebral Shunt," Wikipedia (https://en.wikipedia.org/wiki/Cerebral_shunt)

Gastroenterology: "…the study of the normal function and diseases of the esophagus, stomach, small intestine, colon and rectum, pancreas, gallbladder, bile ducts, and liver."[6] "It involves a detailed understanding of the normal action (physiology) of the gastrointestinal organs including the movement of material through the stomach and intestine (motility), the digestion and absorption of nutrients into the body, removal of waste from the system, and the function of the liver as a digestive organ…. In essence, all normal activity and disease of the digestive organs is part of the study of gastroenterology."[7]

Gastrostomy tube (also called a **G-tube**): "…a tube inserted through the belly that brings nutrition directly to the stomach. It's one of the ways doctors can make sure kids who have trouble eating get the fluid and calories they need."[8]

Geneticist: a person "…who studies genes, including how they are inherited, mutated, activated, or deactivated. They often study the role that genes play in disease and health."[9]

Heparin: "…an anticoagulant (blood thinner) that prevents the formation of blood clots"[10]; "…used to treat and prevent blood clots caused by certain medical conditions or medical procedures."[11]

Hollow visceral myopathy: "…a rare clinical entity characterized by impaired intestinal function in the absence of mechanical occlusion.

[6] "Gastroenterology," Northpointe Health (https://www.northpointehealth.org/services/gastroenterology/)

[7] "What is Gastroenterology?," American Collage of Gastroenterology (https://gi.org/patients/gi-health-and-disease/what-is-a-gastroenterologist/)

[8] "Gastrosomy Tube (G-Tube)," Kidshealth.org (https://kidshealth.org/en/parents/g-tube.html)

[9] "What is a Geneticist?," Environmentalscience.org (https://www.environmentalscience.org/career/geneticist)

[10] "Heparin (Flush)," Michigan Medicine (https://www.uofmhealth.org/health-library/d07385a1)

[11] "Heparin (Injection)," eMedicine Health (https://www.emedicinehealth.com/drug-heparin/article_em.htm)

It can affect the smooth muscle of the whole or segments of the gastrointestinal tract and occasionally the urinary tract."[12]

Hydrocephalus: "...the buildup of fluid in the cavities (ventricles) deep within the brain. The excess fluid increases the size of the ventricles and puts pressure on the brain. Cerebrospinal fluid normally flows through the ventricles and bathes the brain and spinal column. But the pressure of too much cerebrospinal fluid associated with hydrocephalus can damage brain tissues and cause a range of impairments in brain function."[13]

Ileostomy: an opening in the belly (abdominal wall) that's made during surgery. "The end of the ileum (the lowest part of the small intestine) is brought through this opening to form a stoma, usually on the lower right side of the abdomen."[14]

Intestinal pseudo-obstruction: "...a rare condition with symptoms that resemble those caused by a **blockage**, or **obstruction**, of the intestines, also called the **bowel**. ...the symptoms are due to nerve or muscle problems that affect the movement of food, fluid, and air through the intestines."[15]

Kidney stones: "...hard deposits made of minerals and salts that form inside your kidneys. ... Kidney stones form when your urine contains more crystal-forming substances—such as calcium, oxalate and uric

---

[12] S.H.T. Zaidi, M. Arif, & Z. Zaidi, 2003, "Hollow Visceral Myopathy in a 5-Year-Old Boy: A Case Report," *Journal of the Pakistan Medical Association* 53(2):1 (https://jpma. org.pk/article-details/2073).

[13] "Hydrocephalus," Mayo Clinic (https://www.mayoclinic.org/diseases-conditions/ hydrocephalus/symptoms-causes/syc-20373604)

[14] "Ileostomy Guide," United Ostomy Associations of America, Inc., 7 (https://www. ostomy.org/wp-content/uploads/2018/03/IleostomyGuide.pdf)

[15] "Intestinal Pseudo-Obstruction," National Institute of Diabetes and Digestive and Kidney Diseases (https://www.niddk.nih.gov/health-information/digestive-diseases/ intestinal-pseudo-obstruction)

acid—than the fluid in your urine can dilute. At the same time, your urine may lack substances that prevent crystals from sticking together, creating an ideal environment for **kidney stones** to form."[16]

Laparoscopic surgery: also known as "minimally invasive" surgery, this method employs several small incisions, tubes, and tiny cameras transmitting images from inside the abdomen to high-resolution video monitors.[17]

Lithotripsy: "…a way to treat kidney stones without surgery. It is also called extracorporeal shock wave **lithotripsy**, or ESWL. This treatment uses sound waves to break kidney stones into tiny pieces. These pieces can then pass out of the body in the urine."[18]

Meningitis: "…a disease caused by an inflammation of the membranes (meninges) surrounding the brain and spinal cord."[19]

Neurologist: a specialist "…concerned with the study and treatment of disorders of the nervous system. The nervous system is a complex, sophisticated system that regulates and coordinates body activities."[20]

Organ transplantation: "…the surgical removal of a healthy organ from one person and its transplantation into another person whose organ has failed or was injured…."[21]

---

[16] "Kidney Stones," Mayo Clinic (https://www.mayoclinic.org/diseases-conditions/kidney-stones/symptoms-causes/syc-20355755)

[17] "Laparoscopic Surgery—What Is It?," American Society of Colon and Rectal Surgeons (https://www.fascrs.org/patients/disease-condition/laparoscopic-surgery-what-it).

[18] "Lithotripsy: What to Expect at Home," MyHealth.Alberta.ca (https://myhealth.alberta.ca/health/AfterCareInformation/pages/conditions.aspx?HwId=zu2206)

[19] "Meningitis," Columbia University Department of Neurology (http://www.columbianeurology.org/neurology/staywell/document.php?id=33921)

[20] "What Is a Neurologist?," University of Rochester Medicine/Highland Hospital (urmc.rochester.edu/highland/departments-centers/neurology/what-is-a-neurologist.aspx)

[21] "What You Need to Know About Organ Transplants," WebMD (https://www.webmd.com/a-to-z-guides/organ-transplant-overview#1)

Pager (also known as a beeper): "…a wireless telecommunications device that receives and displays alphanumeric or voice messages."[22]

Pancreatic insufficiency: "…a condition in which the **pancreas** is not able to produce and/or transport enough digestive enzymes to break down food in the intestine."[23]

Pediatric ophthalmologist: an eye doctor for children

Placenta previa: "…when a baby's placenta partially or totally covers the mother's cervix—the outlet for the uterus. **Placenta previa** can cause severe bleeding during pregnancy and delivery. If you have **placenta previa,** you might bleed throughout your pregnancy and during your delivery."[24]

Psychologist: a specialist who "…studies how we think, feel, and behave from a scientific viewpoint and applies this knowledge to help people understand, explain and change their behaviour."[25]

Spina bifida: "…a birth defect that occurs when the spine and **spinal** cord don't form properly. It falls under the broader category of neural tube defects. The neural tube is the embryonic structure that eventually develops into the baby's brain and **spinal** cord and the tissues that enclose them."[26]

---

[22] "Pager," Wikipedia (en.wikipedia.org/wiki/Pager)

[23] "What is Pancreatic Insufficiency?," Lab Tests Online (https://labtestsonline.org/conditions/pancreatic-insufficiency)

[24] "Placenta Previa," Mayo Clinic (https://www.mayoclinic.org/diseases-conditions/placenta-previa/symptoms-causes/syc-20352768)

[25] "What is a Psychologist?," Canadian Psychological Association (https://cpa.ca/public/whatisapsychologist/)

[26] "Spina Bifida," May Clinic (https://www.mayoclinic.org/diseases-conditions/spina-bifida/symptoms-causes/syc-20377860)

Total parenteral nutrition (TPN): "...a method of feeding that bypasses the gastrointestinal tract. Fluids are [injected] into a vein to provide most of the nutrients the body needs."[27]

Transplant list: a list of patients waiting for organs.

Ultrasound: "...used to detect changes in the appearance... of organs, tissues, and vessels," and to "detect abnormal masses, such as tumors. In an **ultrasound** examination, a transducer both sends the sound waves and records the echoing waves."[28]

Urology: "...the field of medicine that focuses on diseases of the urinary tract."[29]

---

[27] "Total Parenteral Nutrition—Infants," Medline Plus (https://medlineplus.gov/ency/article/007239.htm)

[28] "Ultrasound," Trego County—Lemke Memorial Hospital (http://www.tclmh.org/services/radiology/ultrasound)

[29] "Faces of Healthcare: What Is a Urologist?," Healthline (https://www.healthline.com/health/what-is-a-urologist)

RESOURCES

To listen to Darryl's interview with Anna Jaworski, visit the following website:
https://www.blogtalkradio.com/hearttoheartwithanna/2018/07/24/
multiple-organ-transplant-due-to-gastric-intestinal-pseudo-obstruction

There are now about one hundred cases of Darryl and Owen's condition worldwide. For more information, visit the following website:
https://rarediseases.org/rare-diseases/chronic-intestinal-pseudo-obstruction/

For disabled children under age eighteen, contact the Easter Seals Society (easterseals.ca) and the Ministry of Community and Social Services in your province.

For disabled children over eighteen years of age, contact the March of Dimes (www.marchofdimes.ca).

About the Author

Sandra Wallis lives in Sarnia, Ontario, Canada with Wayne, her husband of forty-two years. Her four children and five grandchildren bring her much joy as she is now retired from a customer service representative position with a major hotel chain.

Sandra was born in Toronto to an Irish Catholic war bride and a Canadian Protestant father who served in the Canadian Armed Forces. She has one brother who is five years older. Sandra graduated from the University of Western Ontario as a bilingual administrative assistant, and spent two months at Trois Pistoles, Quebec living with a family, as well as six months near Lyon, France as an "au pair."

Sandra enjoys sewing, reading, baking, photography, and travelling. She belongs to a sewing group called "Quilts of Valour" that makes quilts for veterans. She finds this very rewarding. Her passion is growing oriental poppies, especially red ones, and she enjoys going camping with her grown children in Algonquin Park.